Using Technology
Wisely

The Keys to Success
in Schools

Harold Wenglinsky

Teachers College, Columbia University
New York and London

Published by Teachers College Press, 1234 Amsterdam Avenue, New York, NY 10027

Library of Congress Cataloging-in-Publication Data

Wenglinsky, Harold
  Using technology wisely : the keys to success in schools / Harold Wenglinsky
    p. cm.
  Includes bibliographical references and index.
  ISBN 0-8077-4584-7 (cloth) — ISBN 0-8077-4583-9 (pbk.)
    1. Educational technology. 2. Academic achievement
  I. Title
  LB1028.3.W42 2005
  371.33 22   2005041704

ISBN 0-8077-4583-9 (paper)
ISBN 0-8077-4584-7 (cloth)

Printed on acid-free paper

Manufactured in the United States of America
12 11 10 09 08 07 06 05   8 7 6 5 4 3 2 1

To Maria and M.J.

Contents

Acknowledgments

I would like to acknowledge the many people who contributed to the writing and publication of this book. First of all, I would like to thank Craig Jerald of the Education Trust. As a senior editor at *Education Week*, he came up with the idea that it might be possible to use NAEP data to find out if various aspects of technology use were related to student performance. His vision led to the publication of my report *Does It Compute? The Relationship Between Educational Technology and Student Achievement in Mathematics* (Wenglinsky, 1998). A summary of the high points of the study appeared in *Technology Counts 1998* (see Archer, 2000). For his masterful write-up of the study, and his patience with my technical jargon in explaining the study, I want to thank Andrew Trotter along with the other folks at *Education Week* who assisted, including editor-in-chief Virginia Edwards and senior editor Erik Fatemi. I would also like to thank Cheryl Lemke from the Milken Exchange on Educational Technology, who was highly involved in the development of the *Technology Counts* project.

It is this study of mathematics that inspired the additional work included here in science and reading, as well as the case histories. For their comments and input at various stages of the project, I would like to thank Henry Jay Becker at the University of California at Irvine; Ronald Anderson at the University of Minnesota; Ellen Mandinach, research director at the Center for Children and Technology; Christopher Dede at Harvard University; and Kathleen Fulton, recently director of the Web-based Education Commission. I would also like to thank those who let me visit their schools or look at their students' work, including Bruce Goldberg of Co-nect, David Grant at King Middle School, and Todd Wynward at Roots and Wings Community School. Finally, I would like to thank Brian Ellerbeck, Erica DaCosta, and Lynn Raimondo at Teachers College Press, who with their detailed comments, support, and most of all patience, made this a much better book than it would have been otherwise. Nonetheless, any errors of fact or interpretation contained in this book are solely my responsibility.

INTRODUCTION

The Pros and Cons of Educational Technology

For the last 40 years, policymakers and educational researchers have argued about whether computers have a productive role to play in the classroom. As early as the 1960s, educators introduced mainframes and minicomputers into classrooms; then in the 1970s and 1980s personal computers (PCs) began to work their way in; and by the 1990s the Internet and multimedia technologies, such as CD-ROM and computer-based audio and video, made it to schools across the country. As has always been the case when new technologies are introduced into a new environment, school technology had its supporters and detractors. Some policymakers sought to attract funding, both from government sources and the private sector, to improve the ratio of computers to students and ultimately the ratio of Internet and multimedia-capable computers to students. Not only did federal, state, and local governments increasingly support such efforts during the 1980s and 1990s, but the private sector added many of its own funds as well. Governments believed, as a matter of public policy, that students needed to be comfortable with computers to succeed in the job market, and businesses saw computers in the classroom as a way to increase demand for computers in the home and in other businesses. On the other hand, some have questioned this headlong rush to wire the schools. Educational researchers such as Larry Cuban, Jane Healy, and Todd Oppenheimer have raised questions about the educational benefits of computers: Do they in fact help students learn more? Are there ways in which computers are potentially damaging? In response to these critiques and the growing fiscal difficulties that states and the federal government are facing, there are now efforts by some policymakers to rein in their support to bring technology to the classroom. Maine has recently cut back its highly ambitious initiative to give students laptops. And the technology director of the Bush administration, John Bailey, while remaining generally supportive, is taking a low-key approach, in contrast to Linda Roberts, his strongly pro-technology predecessor in the Clinton administration.

Debates about technology and its introduction to institutions are at least as old as the Industrial Revolution, if not older. The first country to industrialize, that is, to move from an agricultural to a factory-based economy, was Britain during the late eighteenth and early nineteenth centuries. Advocates of industrialization, such as Lord Macaulay, believed that technology was going to provide the cure for all of the ills of British society. Rural overpopulation? Bring farm laborers to the city, and they can work in factories. Famines, sickness, and high mortality rates? Technology could increase agricultural productivity while also providing medicine to the sick. A lack of consumer goods? Technology could bring luxuries within the grasp of middle-class people through mass production. But many British citizens were not so sanguine about the benefits of technology. Referred to as *Luddites* after their leader Henry Ludd, Englishmen (and women) went to many of the newly created factory towns and burned the factories to the ground. In their view, technology was taking away their jobs. During the off-season, farmers traditionally engaged in crafts to supplement their income; but now the yarn that they spun was giving way to the factory jenny. The conflict reached violent proportions, leading to brawls between Luddites and militia in numerous towns, until ultimately, in 1819, the Duke of Wellington, hero of Waterloo, ordered his troops to open fire on a band of Luddites in what was dubbed the battle of "Peterloo."

While the contemporary debate on educational technology has hardly reached those proportions, the arguments are surprisingly familiar. Many of the advocates of technology do indeed see it as a method for enhancing school productivity through reducing the role of and perhaps eliminating teachers in the classroom. Two technology advocates exemplify this view. Seymour Papert emerged in the 1970s as an advocate for teaching students computer programming, arguing that students who used his favorite programming language, LOGO, would learn how to think at a higher level of abstraction and would ultimately be able to teach themselves. Thus the ability of computers to raise the conceptual level of student cognition would lead to the replacement of the teacher by the computer.

> Nothing is more ridiculous than the idea that this technology can be used to improve school. It is going to displace school and the way we have understood school. Of course, there will be, we hope, places where children will come together with other people and will learn. But I think that the very nature, the fundamental nature, of school that we see in this process is coming to an end. (Papert quoted in Oppenheimer, 2003, p. 20)

Before Papert, Patrick Suppes offered a very different vision of how computers could dispossess teachers. Starting in the 1960s, Suppes developed computer programs that could be installed on computers and provide a series of exercises for students to complete. This approach, known as computer-assisted instruction (CAI), did not require students to do any programming. Instead, the programs functioned more or less like worksheets. But unlike worksheets, they could be used to take up more and more class time, until they supplanted the teacher. For instance, an evaluation of Suppes's CAI software at the end of the 1980s found that "teachers were tending to use the program as a dumping place....the CAI drilling routines relieved teachers of having to teach" (Komoski quoted in Oppenheimer, 2003, p. 31). Thus, with two very different visions of how technology should be used, Papert and Suppes both saw it as a replacement for teachers, who were the most expensive (and, in their view, unproductive) resource in the school.

Not surprisingly, opponents of technology picked up on the notion that technology would replace the school and held that this would be a bad thing. Some argued that computers reduced opportunities for students to socialize and exchange ideas with one another. In *Fool's Gold* (Cordes & Miller, 2000), the National Association for the Education of Young Children focused on elementary school students, arguing that such students needed a high level of interaction with one another throughout the day or they would become developmentally delayed. Others argued that school computers were bad for teachers. As Larry Cuban has argued, teachers will either ignore computers or do precisely what

Suppes describes: leave students in front of them and not engage in instruction. In his view, some form of teacher-student interaction is critical for student learning.

The problem with this whole debate is that it is so polarized that it bears no relation to how schools are using, or should use, computers in the classroom. Compare the Luddites of 1811. They were wrong when they thought that technology would take away their jobs. It did change the nature of their work, and factory work did turn out to be highly alienating and tedious. But factories actually created more jobs, not fewer; and this was no small matter when the lack of agricultural jobs—due to the enclosure movement, not technology—had been causing high rural unemployment. In addition, as Macaulay projected, industrialization raised the standard of living, with the working class gaining access to goods that only the gentry and aristocracy would have had in an earlier day.

Similarly, and contrary to the arguments of both advocates and opponents of technology, school computers have not replaced teachers, but instead have given them an opportunity to be more productive. I say "opportunity" because some teachers choose to take advantage of computers and some do not. Few teachers have abrogated their authority and teaching responsibilities in favor of a PC. Rather, teachers generally have their students use their computers anywhere from an hour a day to an hour a week to complete a variety of tasks. Depending upon the teacher, students spend more or less time on the computer, but never so much as to take up even half the class time on a regular basis. And much of the time students spend alone with computers is at home; work done with computers in class is usually done with teachers. The nature of the activity also varies. Some teachers tend toward the Suppes-like vision of technology, having students do automated drills on the computer. Others tend toward a more Papertian vision, using computers to solve complex problems that raise the overall ability of students to think abstractly and problem solve.

What determines the way in which students use computers? While many factors are at play, the most important are how the computer fits into the teacher's overall belief system regarding teaching and what other pedagogical techniques teachers use to cover the material. This is the key point of this book: Educational technology needs to be understood not as an isolated event, but as a piece in the puzzle of how teachers teach and students learn. The reason for this follows from the notion that computers do not replace teachers. Because they are just a tool, computers will perform a specific role in the classroom. Teachers and students negotiate what this role is and fit it into the other activities that occur in the classroom. In a Suppes-like classroom, a teacher might lecture on how to solve for x and then have the students solve three similar problems on the computer. In a more Papertian environment, a class might begin with students being given data on daily temperatures and asked to represent them with a graph on the computer. The teacher might then discuss the various potential representations with the students, showing the advantages of labeling the axes certain ways and addressing issues of scale. Thus, understanding the role of technology in the classroom requires an understanding of these two approaches to learning that I have called "Suppes-like" and "Papertian," which are commonly termed *didactic* and *constructivist*.

TWO TYPES OF TEACHING

Both educational research and educational philosophy generally hold that teaching beliefs and practices conform to one of two types of pedagogies, the didactic or the constructivist. The didactic approach is the more traditional one. It views student learning as going through a linear progression from facts to analyses of these facts and from basic skills such as numbers and operations to more advanced skills such as solving complex problems through analysis of real data. While the traditional view believes in this progression, it defers the advanced skills until later and later in the child's development, either to college or to advanced placement courses in high school. For the most part, students in elementary and secondary schools lack sufficient knowledge to engage in analysis and synthesis, and consequently, except for the most advanced students, most time should be spent on conveying knowledge. This notion of what students learn suggests certain didactic beliefs about how students should learn it. For example, students begin learning a given subject at basically the same point; either the student knows how to sound out words or not. Thus instruction should not be customized to a particular student or subgroup of students; rather they should be moved forward at roughly the same rate. Further, the teacher should make the key decisions about what to cover, when to cover it, and how to convey it, in the belief that teachers are the ones full of knowledge, while students are receptacles of that knowledge. Finally, student progress should be assessed primarily through tests that determine whether students have the knowledge and skills covered in that unit. All of these didactic beliefs suggest a classroom in which teachers lecture about an algorithm to solve routine problems (or, in the case of reading, sound out the relevant words by breaking them into their constituent phonemes) and students then apply the algorithm to a series of problems where the numbers or words change, but the structure remains the same.

The constructivist approach is the polar opposite. Rather than viewing students as developing linearly from basic to advanced skills, this approach holds that basic skills almost always have to be embedded in advanced skills, both because the advanced problems are more exciting for students to learn and because it helps them get the "big picture." For example, while there is no doubt that students need a unit on the times tables, this can be sandwiched into a lesson on the meaning of multiplication and its visual representation. Thus development is an iterative process, where basic skills are juxtaposed with more advanced skills. Ideally, these advanced skills—referred to as "higher order thinking skills"—frame instruction from K–12, and can be defined as the movement back and forth between the abstract, such as a law of Newtonian physics, and the concrete, such as what happens to a person when their car instantly decelerates from 35 miles per hour to zero. Like the didactic approach, the constructivist beliefs suggest a certain set of practices. First and foremost, teaching should be highly customized. Students come to the classroom with certain ways of knowing things (sociologists refer to this as the "social construction of knowledge"). Thus a Latina student may absorb scientific concepts in a different way than a Native American male. Indeed, this customization should be so extensive that teachers are viewed as facilitating student construction of knowledge. According to the colloquial phrase often associated with this phenomenon, the teacher is not the "sage on the stage, but the guide on the side." In terms of assessment, the constructivist approach avoids testing. Student work completed during the course of normal class time and collected in portfolios can be used by the teacher to assess student learning. The ongoing work can be punctuated with student projects that are due at set times. One corollary of these practices is that students engage in work in three formats: As a whole class, in small groups, or as individuals. A typical classroom might have students divided into four groups working on projects, with the teacher walking around and assisting each group when it gets "stuck."

It is important to note that the key distinction between the two pedagogies is that of lower order versus higher order thinking skills and not student versus teacher initiation of work. According to didactic pedagogy's view, students best learn basic skills by spending most of their time on learning them; if students are having trouble learning, the solution is to give them more drills or repeat the same information. According to constructivist pedagogy's view, students should think as abstractly as possible, and this in turn is facilitated through exposure to the most concrete and practical illustrations of concepts; if students are having trouble learning a concept, the solution is to give them an example from a different context; and if they are having trouble problem solving, then the form in which the concept is framed needs to be changed for those particular students (as opposed to the students for whom the first framing is more convivial) Student versus teacher initiation of work is not always a distinction between the pedagogies. While, by and large, the iterative approach to the abstract and concrete is best served by having students direct the work, there are examples in the literature where teacher direction has proven more successful, such as in the application of metacognitive skills to reading. Metacognitive skills are those that describe what the reader is doing when making inferences from the text. Research indicates that a technique known as "reciprocal teaching" works well in this regard. First, the teacher states explicitly what he or she is doing in reading the passage. Then a student models what he or she is doing for a peer. Then the peer reciprocates. This technique ultimately gives control to the student, but only after the teacher has given the metacognitive greater concreteness.

In my own teaching, I have found that the constructivist approach of moving iteratively from concepts to their illustrations in problems is crucial for student learning, as is responding to the heterogeneity of student learning styles. I have typically relied on problem-based learning approaches to teaching, in which students read heavily conceptual articles or books and then divide into small groups to solve practical problems. Admittedly, I teach college students; but in my frequent observations of K–12 classrooms, I have seen that constructivist approaches are superior there as well.

FITTING EDUCATIONAL TECHNOLOGY INTO PRACTICE

I have also found that technology is a better fit with the constructivist approach than the didactic. In didactic approaches, the computer very often becomes a substitute for the teacher or other materials. At the risk of dating myself, I offer the following analogy. In the movie *Fast Times at Ridgemont High*, which represented classrooms in the late 1970s before the computer revolution fully took hold in the schools, one of the teachers was nicknamed Ditto because he handed out worksheets run off on a Ditto machine to all students at the beginning of class, read the newspaper to himself, and then collected the sheets at the end of the class. In a didactic classroom the computerized analogue to Ditto is the teacher who has the students walk into a computer lab at the beginning of class, sit down in front of their computers, and do drills while the teacher sits in front of his or her computer and plays solitaire. In this situation, the computer is at best a substitute for a worksheet, and at worst increases the likelihood that the teacher will get away with such a lackluster performance because he or she appears to be at the technological cutting edge. What might be unacceptable on paper seems fine on a video screen.

In concert with the constructivist approach, computers become one of many tools students can use to concretize concepts. The role of the teacher is to try to convey the initial abstraction to students and help students try to convey it to one another. To make the concept concrete, students and teachers could choose from a variety of strategies. In chemistry, they might create solutions in a laboratory. In civics, they might go on a field trip to meet a local public official. And in geography, they might use the Internet to collect information about a place and produce a set of slides that visually represents the environment, culture, history, and demography of it. Because the constructivist focus on problem solving means that students do most of the work, computers only replace teachers to the extent that teachers have given students the freedom to make their own mistakes and successes on a computer as well as on a field trip or in a lab. (For some vivid examples of how this can work, see Linn & His, 2000.)

The truly challenging question for those of us who advocate a constructivist role for educational technology is this: What is the valued-added of the technology above and beyond good teaching? Let us grant, for the moment, that constructivist approaches are more effective than didactic ones for most students in most settings. Let us therefore view teachers who are well able to apply the constructivist approach as effective teachers. Since they can select any number of tools to achieve their goals, why are computers a necessary option? The answer, I believe, is that learning consists of three pieces, the teacher, the student, and the medium; and it is not possible to separate one out from the others. Think of computers as akin to language. Teachers and students use language to communicate with one another. That language imposes some constraints on what the two groups can say, but it also provides a whole host of opportunities. Computers, field trips, and chemistry labs are similar in that they provide what are referred to as "teachable moments" where, through doing something, a student finally makes sense out of something the teacher was trying to convey. Just as an effective teacher needs to have five different phrases for defining a given concept, the teacher needs to have multiple media for illustrating it; and in fact, computers in and of themselves provide multiple media for learning.

THE FOCUS OF THIS BOOK

This book presents what is, I believe, a somewhat unusual take on technology, namely that it is neither inherently good nor bad, but its value depends upon how it is used. If used in a constructivist fashion, it is a useful tool; and if used in a didactic fashion, it is worthless, or even destructive, burying students in the "drill-and-kill" model that turns all but the greatest of automatons off learning. Therefore, educational leaders should keep the technology they have and even increase it, as long as they steer their teachers toward constructivist practice. None of the schools described in this book as successful with technology use it in a vacuum. The teacher has an overall plan of how to teach students in a constructivist manner, and technology is one component.

In addition to its unusual take, this book makes use of data in a different way than other books on the subject of educational technology. Most are full of anecdotes and case histories that support the author's point of view for or against technology, and there is a chapter in this book that illustrates the didactic and constructivist uses of technology. A case history approach, however, cannot demonstrate the effectiveness of a particular technology use, so another chapter of this book goes on to test the anecdotes using real national numbers. How often are computers used in constructivist and didactic ways? Which students are most likely to be exposed to which approaches? Outside of using technology, which approach raises test scores most, the constructivist or didactic? And, in concert with using technology, which approach has the most positive effect on test scores? I answer these questions in the subjects of math, science, and reading by using the National Assessment of Educational Progress (NAEP) for 1996, 1998, and 2000, tests administered to national samples of 4th, 8th, and 12th graders by the federal government. Known as "the nation's report card," it is used to track student performance over time and between demographic groups. In addition to the test, questionnaires are administered to students and their teachers. Thus it is possible to gauge the effect of various pedagogical uses of technology on achievement, taking into account other characteristics of students and teachers. This is a powerful tool for generalizing to the entire country how technology is linked to achievement, aside from local causes of educational phenomena such as school region, the predominant demographics of students, or the educational backgrounds of teachers.

Thus focusing on the effectiveness of various uses of technology, the book explores the subject from several angles. Chapter 1 provides the policy context for educational technology, juxtaposing it with other movements for educational reform. Chapter 2 reviews the existing research on educational technology, both pro and con. In Chapter 3 some case studies of didactic and constructivist uses of technology are presented, and Chapter 4 puts numbers to these anecdotes, showing which practices are most prevalent and which are most effective. The last chapter sums up what can be learned from these numbers and offers some suggestions for policymakers and practitioners. An appendix for researchers provides the technical details of how the study was conducted.

KEY POINTS

- For centuries, policymakers have debated the merits of introducing a particular technology into a particular environment. Now the hotly contested question is whether computers belong in the classroom.
- Teaching tends to be one of two types: didactic, in which students are taught basic skills primarily through having the teacher provide the knowledge and students receive it; or constructivist, in which students are taught complex problem-solving skills in an iterative process that moves from abstractions to concrete examples, where students control most of the learning process.
- The effectiveness of educational technology is enmeshed in the kind of pedagogy employed. Constructivist uses of technology help students learn better than they would otherwise, whereas didactic uses of technology make the technology useless or even damaging.

CHAPTER 1

Standards, Technology, and Teaching: Three Movements for Improving the Schools

The 1990s have been noteworthy in education policy for the emergence of three interrelated movements for school improvement: the standards movement, the technology movement, and the movement to improve teacher quality. The first of these held that students needed to be held to higher academic standards; the second, that technology could be a crucial tool in helping students meet these higher standards; and the third, that standards needed to be raised for teachers if they were going to be raised for students. The fundamental interconnectedness of these three movements means not only that policymakers need to provide technology for schools and improve teacher quality to raise academic standards, but that they need to connect improvements in teacher quality to increasing technology use in the classroom. Policymakers can make this connection in two ways. They can provide professional development in computer use to teachers so that they are comfortable with technology. But they also need to provide professional development to teachers in subject matter and pedagogy so that teachers can think of sophisticated ways to use computers and envision how computers will fit into the menu of pedagogical techniques teachers employ every day.

Over the last 2 decades, federal, state, and local policymakers and business leaders have pushed on three fronts to save America's schools from mediocrity. In the wake of the 1983 report, *A Nation at Risk* (National Commission on Excellence in Education, 1983), these leaders have scrambled to find ways to improve the performance of U.S. students. The standards movement, which emerged directly from the report, sought to develop academic standards that measured what students should know. By making these standards higher than the minimum competency standards of the 1970s, the standards movement sought to raise expectations for all students. During the late 1980s and early 1990s, policymakers and business leaders identified an important tool for improving student performance: educational technology. In their view, technology such as personal computers and networks was revolutionizing the workplace, unleashing major productivity gains that resulted in an unprecedented period of economic growth in the 1990s. By using such media in the schools, they believed that they could initiate similar gains in educational productivity, leading students to meet the new, challenging academic standards. In the mid-1990s, however, it became clear that one piece was missing from school reform: the improvement of the teaching force. In a 1996 report, *What Matters Most* (National Commission on Teaching and America's Future, 1996), policymakers and business leaders agreed that just as the human capital needs of the nation's workforce were increasing in response to the intellectual demands of technology, so too would the needs of the educational workforce. Regarding technology specifically, teachers who had been in the system for years using chalk and blackboards had to be retrained to use technology if the desired productivity gains were to materialize. Technology aside, teachers needed to be prepared both in their college years and in on-the-job training to meet higher standards if it was going to be feasible for students to meet higher standards. Thus the three movements of raising academic standards, introducing technology, and improving teacher quality proved to be related to one another, and ultimately policymakers who pushed for one of these movements had to push for them all.

That said, at their inception the three movements suffered from a certain vagueness that made it difficult to see what changes they were trying to leverage in the classroom. On the face of it, the movements were neutral about the central issue surrounding instruction: Should it be didactic or constructivist in its focus? The standards movement proved minimally prescriptive in this regard. While some national professional organizations came out with standards that were primarily constructivist in nature (e.g., the National Council of Teachers of Mathematics and the National Science Teachers Association), individual states chose standards that were constructivist or didactic depending upon the political winds of the day. Reading standards in California veered from highly constructivist approaches to highly didactic ones. Maryland chose constructivist standards in most subjects, whereas, just across the Potomac, Virginia chose didactic ones. The implementation of educational technology reflected a similar pedagogical neutrality. Some programs, such as Apple Computers of Tomorrow, were vigorously constructivist, whereas others involved computer-assisted instruction as a series of drill-and-practice routines. And even the idea of improving teacher quality had its constructivist and didactic spins. Most national organizations, including the National Council on the Accreditation of Teacher Education, took a constructivist spin, but alternative organizations of a didactic nature arose. For instance, in the area of state policymaking, liberal to centrist policymakers joined the Council for Chief State School Officers, which had constructivist leanings, whereas conservative policymakers founded the basic-skills–oriented Educational Leadership Council.

The vagueness of the three movements creates two hurdles to their successful realization. First, their vagueness creates the potential for them to be inconsistent and at cross-purposes, depending upon the way the political wind is blowing. As discussed in the previous chapter, the key to effective technology use is to have teachers make use of it in a constructivist fashion as one of many media. But if teachers are moving in a constructivist direction and software is moving in a didactic one, then teachers will lack the software they need to meet their instructional goals. The second hurdle to the successful use of educational technology is that the movements may develop consistently, but this consistency may be of a didactic nature. What if standards, software, and teachers all move in the direction of teaching basic skills, neglecting the higher order thinking skills that research shows are critical to student intellectual development? Then, frankly, the educational technology movement, and school reform in general, will fail. Schools are supposed to prepare students to participate in the workforce, and that workforce is not neutral about pedagogy. The workforce of the twenty-first-century values independent decision making, complex problem solving, teamwork, and ongoing performance appraisal—all components of a constructivist, not a didactic pedagogy. For the three movements to succeed, they all need to be constructivist in their orientation.

Overall, data on student performance have not brought good news regarding the impact of these three movements during the 1990s. NAEP scores indicate that the vast majority of students are not proficient in math, science, or reading, at either the 4th, 8th, or 12th grades. Performance in reading has remained unchanged, and performance in math and science has improved only slightly (National Center for Education Statistics [NCES], 2000). On a scale from 0 to 500, mean reading scores between 1988 and 1999 for 9-year-olds went from 212 to 212, for 13-year-olds from 257 to 259, and for 17-year-olds from 290 to 288, none a statistically significant difference. In math, between 1990 and 1999, mean scores for 9-year-olds went from 230 to 232, for 13-year-olds from 270 to 276, and for 17-year-olds from 305 to 308, all significant but extremely modest increases. In science, between 1990 and 1999, mean scores for 9-year-olds remained at 229, but for 13-year-olds went from 255 to 256, and for 17-year-olds from 290 to 295, only the last of the three being statistically significant.

International comparisons have been similarly discouraging. The Third International Math and Science Study (TIMSS) tested the performance of students in countries all over the world, as well as surveying students and teachers. According to TIMSS, U.S. students are somewhat above average in 4th grade, in the middle by 8th grade, and among the lowest performers in the 12th grade (NCES, 1996b, 1997, 1998).

To this extent, then, the three movements have not fulfilled their promise. Despite massive investments in technology, students in the technology-rich classrooms of the late 1990s learned little more than their counterparts did in the late 1980s. Increased access to technology cannot enhance performance without an effective teaching force and high standards. And, as the TIMSS research revealed, the U.S. teaching force is primarily a didactic one, whereas that of one of the highest performing countries, Japan, is a constructivist one. Stigler and Hiebert (1999) analyzed videotapes of classes in the United States, Germany, and Japan. They found that U.S. teachers cover a great breadth of material, but with little depth, whereas Japanese teachers cover material in depth, but with little breadth. U.S. teachers present a single algorithm to students of how to solve a given problem and then have them solve the same problem over and over again with slightly different numbers. Japanese teachers introduce a complex problem and give students the opportunity to solve it in various ways; they then discuss the various solutions and relate them to the underlying mathematical concepts. U.S. teachers present proofs to their students, whereas Japanese teachers have the students derive the proofs. While Stigler and Hiebert's book can hardly prove the superiority of constructivism by associating its prevalence with high student test scores in Japan (other factors may be at work), it shows that the school reform movements in the United States, to succeed, must give up their pedagogical neutrality. They must recognize that constructivist teachers are effective teachers, constructivist technology is effective technology, and constructivist standards should be the yardstick for student performance. Yet, to maintain elite political consensus, policymakers and business leaders have steered clear of this view, not taking sides in the pedagogical wars.

THE STANDARDS MOVEMENT

The story of the standards movement has often been told (Ravitch, 1995; Tucker & Codding, 1998). It began with a series of national reports, in particular *A Nation at Risk*, produced by a panel convened by secretary of education Terrell Bell. The report concluded that the education system was producing a generation of mediocrities. "If an unfriendly foreign power had attempted to impose on America the mediocre educational performance that exists today, we might well have viewed it as an act of war" (National Commission on Excellence in Education, 1983, p. 1). The report called for policymakers to raise expectations of what students should be expected to learn. In the wake of sustained media coverage of this and other reports, many state governors heeded the call to raise standards. The most aggressive action was taken in southern states, where governors Lamar Alexander, Richard Riley, and Bill Clinton passed elaborate education reform packages. The actions by governors culminated in 1989 in a national education summit in Charlottesville, Virginia, jointly convened by the White House and the National Governors Association. Soon after, Lamar Alexander, by then secretary of education, promulgated America 2000, a plan to formulate a series of standards and a series of goals the U.S. education system would be expected to meet by 2000. The key notion in this plan was that the standards would be national, but not federal. The federal government would not draft the standards but rather give grants to professional bodies representing various subject areas to draft standards. The model used was the mathematics standards, drafted by the National Council of Teachers of Mathematics (NCTM) in 1989.

America 2000 went through a number of versions before it was enacted into law by Congress as Goals 2000 in 1994. The act involved content, performance, and opportunity-to-learn (or school-delivery), standards and assessments. *Content standards* refer to the material students are expected to know in various subjects. Implicit in the content standards is the idea that they include all material students need to continue on to college. Content standards were first operationalized in the NCTM standards of 1989, followed by the science standards of the National Science Teachers Association (NSTA) in 1997 and the very controversial English/language arts standards and history standards. *Performance standards* refer to what precisely students need to be able to do to demonstrate proficiency in a content standard. For instance, if a content standard involved using geometric theorems to understand the lengths and angles of triangles, a performance standard might expect students to be able to apply the Pythagorean theorem to determine the length of a side of a triangle from the lengths of the other sides. *Assessments* are the instruments that ask students questions based upon the performance standards to test their command of these standards. In the geometry example, an assessment item might ask the length of a leg given a hypotenuse of 5 inches and another leg of 3 inches. Performance standards and assessments based on those standards were opposed at the federal level over fears that they would serve as the basis for national tests and, consequently, a national curriculum. Ultimately, no national tests were produced. Finally, *opportunity-to-learn standards* refer to whether schools offer courses covering the material required by the other standards. Some policymakers expanded this definition somewhat to include the availability of resources (money, teachers, training) to support such courses. Opportunity-to-learn standards met a fate similar to that of the national tests, opposed by policymakers who saw them as an opportunity for the federal government to dictate the configuration and resource allocation of districts and schools (Ravitch, 1995).

The passage of Goals 2000, along with the Elementary and Secondary Education Act (ESEA) of 1994, did provide an opportunity for more action at the state level. Governors and business leaders convened a second education summit in 1995 and affirmed their desire to promulgate state standards. They also created the organization Achieve to provide technical assistance to states in the development of standards. By the year 2000, although the education goals had not been reached, all states but one (Iowa) had a set of content standards. Most also had assessments, although these rarely stemmed from state performance standards; such assessments are said to be "not aligned" with state standards. Curricula and teaching practices also remained, by and large, aligned "not with the standards" (American Federation of Teachers, 1999).

The passage of the reauthorization of the Elementary and Secondary Education Act in 2002, known as No Child Left Behind (NCLB), is the culmination of the standards movement. NCLB provided that federal education dollars for disadvantaged students (known as Title I of the ESEA) would be contingent upon states' having standards and assessment plans to measure student performance in the third through eighth grades. The validity of such tests would be evaluated by comparing their results to those of the NAEP tests, given to representative samples of students in each state. In addition, states would be expected to identify *failing schools*, defined as those which did not make adequate yearly progress (AYP) in their test scores. AYP meant not only increases in average school scores but also increases in scores for various demographic subgroups based upon race, socioeconomic status, and other factors. Schools that repeatedly failed to make AYP would have to pay to allow students to attend other public schools, and the schools might even be reconstituted. NCLB thus created enforcement mechanisms for teaching students toward high standards (U.S. Department of Education, 2003c).

As might be imagined, much opposition had sprung up,

on both the left and right, to such an ambitious proposal for educational change, when the basic principles of the Bush proposal for NCLB were disseminated in 2001. The next year Congress was due to reauthorize the Elementary and Secondary Education Act, which had served as the key legislation for federal efforts to help support education in low-income communities since 1965. The Bush administration decided to let Congress take the initiative, asking it to incorporate the key elements of NCLB into the ESEA reauthorization. On the left, opponents argued that ESEA did not provide for sufficient financial resources to provide students with an opportunity to learn; not enough money was available to permit schools to hire a sufficient number of high-quality teachers, to keep class sizes at a reasonable level, and to ensure that an appropriate curriculum was taught. On the right, opponents argued that the legislation amounted to a federal takeover of education, with the federal government dictating what students should learn and how schools should be run. Ultimately, the legislation passed because it took these objections into account to some extent: More money was authorized for education than ever before, and states were allowed to develop their own standards and assessments, thus making their own judgments about whether schools were meeting the standard of adequate yearly progress. (Another concern of the left, the provision of vouchers for private school tuition, which the Bush administration advocated as an alternative to failing public schools, was also eliminated in the final legislation.)

While much of the infrastructure that the standards movement called for has been erected, significant gaps remain. Perhaps the largest is in the area of opportunity to learn. Providing strong incentives for states, schools, and students to meet high standards is no guarantee that they have the capacity to do so; and policymakers and educators do not agree on ways to ensure that they do. Some call for reducing class sizes; others for raising teacher salaries; still others for restructuring school systems through creating charter schools, magnet schools, or small schools.

Two opportunity-to-learn issues received particular attention during the 1990s: educational technology and teacher quality. Many policymakers and educators hold that technology is the single most useful tool for improving schools and ensuring accountability. Others maintain that teacher quality is crucial, because if teachers are not capable of teaching to high standards, students will not learn them. While NCLB addressed these issues as well, it is worthwhile to examine the roots of these movements.

THE EDUCATIONAL TECHNOLOGY MOVEMENT

The movement to bring computers and other new forms of technology to the classroom, like the standards movement, involved three key players: the federal government, state governments, and the private sector. Federal involvement began with the Improving America's Schools Act of 1994, Section 2, Title II, Part A. This portion of the Goals 2000 Act came to be known as the Technology for Education Act of 1994 and called for increased student exposure to technology to help meet the goals:

> Sec. 3111: [T]echnology can produce far greater opportunities for all students to learn to high standards, promote efficiency and effectiveness in education, and help propel our Nation's School Systems into very immediate and dramatic reform, without which our nation will not meet the National Education Goals by the target year 2000. (U.S. Department of Education, 2003b)

In 1996, based upon this act, the Clinton administration unveiled two initiatives: the Technology Literacy Challenge Fund (TLCF) and the Technology Innovation Challenge Grants (TICG). The focus of TLCF was on creating the infrastructure for student technological literacy. The Technology Literacy Challenge consisted of four goals:

1. *Professional development of teachers:* All teachers in the nation will have the training and support they need to help students learn by using computers and the Internet.
2. *Hardware access:* All teachers and students will have modern multimedia computers in their classrooms.
3. *Connectivity:* Every classroom will be connected to the Internet.
4. *Digital content:* Effective software and online learning resources will be an integral part of every school's curriculum.

The TLCF offered $5 billion over 5 years to support states and localities in achieving these goals (U.S. Department of Education, 1996).

The focus of TICG, on the other hand, was to experiment with ways to utilize that technology to improve student subject learning. Consortia of educators, researchers, industrial leaders, and others were to apply for grants for 5-year projects. The first year would be for start-up, the second and third years for refinements and expansions, and the fourth and fifth years for scale-up systemwide. After the fifth year, programs were to be self-sustaining. Grants had to support at least one of the following six activities:

1. Develop technology applications that support school reform.
2. Provide projects to increase student learning, or professional development to support technology use.
3. Enhance school technology infrastructures.
4. Provide professional development to integrate technology into education.
5. Create wide-area networks for access to information outside of schools.
6. Provide educational services for adults. (Merchilinsky, 2001)

Nineteen ninety-six proved to be a watershed year for federal technology initiatives. In the same year, Congress also passed the Telecommunications Act, which called for telecommunications companies to provide funds for schools to obtain Internet access. The companies generally funded the program through imposing surcharges on their customers. Opposition to the program, which had been proposed and supported by the Clinton administration, caused this change to be nicknamed the "Gore Tax" because of the vice president's identification with technology issues. The resulting program, known as "e-rate," was designed to increase Internet access in the schools. The amount of money was capped each year. School districts could apply for Tier I grants, which were for telephone service and basic Internet access. There were generally sufficient funds to support all Tier I grants. Tier II grants were for more elaborate projects, such as wiring classrooms or purchasing servers and routers. Here, high-poverty districts (where more than 75% of students qualified for free or reduced-price lunches) were given preference, with the remaining funds going to somewhat less poor districts. Because the funds applied for ($5.2 billion in 2001) generally exceeded the cap ($2.25 billion in 2001), the less poor districts often did not receive funds for Tier II projects (Trotter, 2000).

A fourth Clinton administration initiative on technology was Preparing Tomorrow's Teachers for Technology (PT3). Launched in 1999, the program supported the activities of consortia—which had to include both institutions of higher education and school districts— to train teachers in technology use. Projects were required to

> create one or more programs that prepare prospective teachers to use advanced technology to prepare all students, including groups of students who are underrepresented in technology-related fields and groups of students who are economically disadvantaged, to meet challenging state and local academic content standards. (U.S. Department of Education, 2004)

Projects also had to have an evaluation component. Permissible projects included faculty development, course restructuring, certification policy changes, online teacher preparation, and electronic portfolios. In total, 400 such grants were offered.

The actions taken by the Clinton administration from 1994 through 1999 were discussed in a pair of influential reports released soon after Clinton's tenure was over: *E-Learning: Putting a World-Class Education at the Fingertips of All Children* (U.S. Department of Education, 2000) and *Moving from Promise to Practice* (Web-Based Education Commission, 2001). The e-learning report evaluated progress toward meeting five goals: (1) student and teacher access to technology, (2) teacher training in the use of technology, (3) student literacy in the use of technology, (4) the availability of strong digital content, and (5) research and evaluation to improve the effectiveness of technology. The report's findings in regard to each of these goals revealed the following needs: (1) greater access to broadband and networks; (2) improved preservice and in-service training in technology for teachers and more technical support so that problems with technology that teachers encounter can be addressed quickly; (3) training for students not only in how to use computers but also in how to develop appropriate problem-solving skills using computers; (4) digitization of more educational materials, the recognition of effective educational software developers, and the greater integration of digital content into curriculum; and (5) a systemic research and evaluation agenda on the application of technology to teaching and learning, including state and local evaluations of technology as well as the dissemination and concrete use of study results.

The Web-Based Commission's report highlighted the impact of e-rate (the growth of online school programs) and expressed concern about the digital divide (the relative lack of computer access experienced by higher poverty schools and their students). It also called for more research on the effectiveness of educational technology, more teacher training, better digital content, and improvements in the quality of Internet access.

In the wake of the four Clinton initiatives (known as the "four pillars") and two reports, the Bush administration has pursued a similar course in its technology plans. Title II of NCLB, Part D, Subparts 1 and 2, provides for an educational technology and state grants program and various national technology activities (U.S. Department of Education, 2003a). Title II notes the importance of technology for enhancing curricula, increasing student achievement and creating job market skills. The legislation also notes the existence of a "digital divide" in access to computers that connect to the Internet, with a 9:1 ratio in high-poverty schools as opposed to a 6:1 ratio in low-poverty schools. Further, with 27% of teachers prepared to integrate technology into instruction, large numbers of teachers are not prepared to use technology.

The educational technology state grants are to supersede the TLCF. The legislation characterized what was new compared to the 1994 legislation as the following points:

- Engages in strategies more heavily immersed in research
- Requires at least 25% of funds to be used for professional development
- Mandates a national study of the conditions under which technology is effective for teaching and learning
- Increases flexibility for how states can use funds

- Requires state technology goals to be aligned with state academic standards
- Provides special grants for districts that (1) are high-poverty, (2) have at least one low-performing school, or (3) need assistance in basic hardware acquisition

In total, 5% of funds go to state-level activities, and of the remainder, half go to districts based upon their share of Title I funds with the rest going to high-need districts. In addition to Title II of NCLB, Title V, Part D, Subpart 2 provides for community technology centers (CTCs). CTCs are designed to develop model programs to demonstrate the effectiveness of technologies in communities. They involve up to 3-year grants to a nongovernmental organization or school district to increase technology access. Federal funds are to be matched.

In terms of actual funding, the Bush plan amounted to a consolidation of the Clinton programs at a similar funding level ("Final Fiscal," 2001). For FY02, Clinton proposed $450,000,000 for TLCF, $136,328,000 for TICG, $10,000,000 for regional technology in education consortia, $191,950,000 for various national technology education activities, $59,318,000 for Star schools, $16,000,000 for ready-to-learn TV, and $8,500,000 for a telecommunications demonstration for mathematics. Bush proposed to consolidate this into the $817,096,000 education state grant program.

Thus the years from 1994 to 2002 represented a continuous effort on the part of the federal government to encourage the use of technology by schools. Substantial funds, typically over $800 million a year, were used to increase the availability of hardware and connectivity at schools in need of it, to increase professional development of teachers, and to increase the quality of educational software and online services. Given the federal government's relatively small financial stake in K–12 education (less than 7%), these efforts are remarkable. Nevertheless, they were paralleled by similar efforts by states and the private sector.

States have also made significant investments in educational technology during this time, and grappled with the issues surrounding standards for teachers and students in the use of technology. Many of these efforts have been in response to federal policy. States that have taken an active role in the e-rate program have had more success in increasing Internet access. For instance, Mississippi negotiated a rate with Bell South so that rural districts pay less than $500 per month for T1 lines, rather than the market rate of $1,200 to $2,000. In some states, however, government involvement in e-rate has been problematic. In Georgia, for instance, many e-rate funds could not be accounted for, leading to an FBI probe. Some states have focused on investments to reduce the digital divide. Thus Florida, Illinois, and Virginia have created after-school computer labs so that students without computers at home can have access. Such labs have proven costly (e.g., $11 million in Illinois). Florida has also invested in creating an online high school, permitting students in schools that do not offer AP courses to take them online; this program cost the state $16 million. Focusing on teachers, Michigan has spent $110 million to furnish each of the state's 90,000 teachers with a laptop or desktop computer (Sandham, 2001).

Perhaps one of the states most committed to educational technology is South Dakota (Borja, 2002). Because the state is so sparsely populated, there is an inherent need for distance learning, in which students learn from dispersed locations, rather than at a single geographical point; technology is a key tool for distance learning because it lets students and teachers communicate and share work over long distances. Like Mississippi, South Dakota negotiated inexpensive connection rates with its local telecommunications companies, Qwest and SDN Communications. The state invested $12 million in high-speed wiring and technical services. It also spent $7 million for broadband host and network support, $1.7 million for audiovisual equipment, and $15 million for 11.5 million feet of CATV wiring and 208,000 feet of fiber optic cable. Later, the state purchased 16,000 new computers from Gateway and Apple and started a statewide network with the capacity to engage in video conferencing. The state then turned its attention to teachers, online testing, and curriculum development. Teachers were able to attend month-long technology academies, receiving a $1,000 stipend and $1,000 to use for classroom technology such as software. To date, 4 out of 10 teachers have participated. Online testing was launched in Grades 3, 6, and 10. The assessments were based upon the state's academic standards and provided substantial diagnostic information to teachers. Finally, the state history textbook was put online and made interactive for fourth graders, an attempt to meld curriculum with digital content.

States have also been promulgating technology standards for students and teachers. As of 2000, 35 states included technology in their academic standards and 4 tested students on them. As for teachers, 27 states require prospective teachers to take courses in technology training, and 7 require prospective teachers to demonstrate technological competence. Of states that have recertification processes for teachers, 4 include a technology component. And 13 states provide incentives to teachers to use technology (Meyer, 2001).

Despite all this activity, states recognize that much more needs to be done. A recent report by the National Association of State Boards of Education (NASBE) notes that "e-learning will improve American education in valuable ways and should be universally implemented as soon as possible" (NASBE, 2001, p. 1). Action, in the view of NASBE, needs to occur in three areas: (1) reengineering the education system to increase technology use, (2) assuring greater equity in access to technology, and (3) providing higher quality instruction in e-learning. State commissions have also called for new policies to increase technology use. The Maryland Mathematics Commission, for instance, noted in its recent report that, despite gains in computer access and use, significant gaps remain. Nearly 50% of classrooms lack Internet access. Less than 10% of schools have a full-time technology coordinator to provide technical support to teachers. One out of 4 teachers cannot browse the Web or use e-mail. And 4 out of 10 teachers do not know how to integrate technology into their curricula. Thus the Maryland Commission finds it crucial to ensure that (1) all students have computer access, (2) prospective teachers be required to demonstrate computer skills, and (3) teachers incorporate technology into the curriculum and practice of math instruction (Maryland Mathematics Commission, 2001).

The private companies, particularly those heavily involved in technology, have been enormously supportive of bringing technology to schools. Perhaps the best known effort is Apple Computers of Tomorrow (ACOT). This program, implemented by Apple Computers in the 1980s, created a series of innovative projects at schools to use computers to teach complex thinking skills

(Sandholtz, Ringstaff, & Dwyer, 1997). In the 1990s Apple and other companies formed a consortium to identify needed technological skills and make recommendations for fulfilling them. Known as the CEO Forum, this organization included representatives from the private sector such as AOL, Apple, Bell South, Compaq, Dell, Hewlett-Packard, Lucent Technologies, Sun Microsystems, and Verizon, as well as some educational organizations including the National Education Association and the National School Boards Association. Between 1997 and 2001, the forum generated a series of four reports on connectivity, professional development of teachers, digital content, and accountability (CEO Forum on Education and Technology, 1997, 1999, 2000, 2001). The reports noted that there had been much progress over the years in getting computers into the classroom (e.g., the student to computer ratio had declined from 10 students per computer to 5 students per computer between 1995 and 2000). It recommended three additional steps. First, policymakers needed to redefine student achievement to include twenty-first-century skills, such as technological competence and problem solving, skills for which computers were vital. Second, federal spending on technology should be doubled. Some of this money should be used to decrease the digital divide, but by 2003 a third of it should be devoted to professional development of teachers and integrating technology into the curriculum. Third, more money should be invested in research and development in order to identify effective educational technology uses.

Individual companies and foundations have also donated funds to increase technology use. The Intel Corporation has donated hardware to school districts in various states. For instance, in the Jordan, Utah, school district, it donated $150,000 for six wireless math/science laboratories, $30,000 for a class in technology product life cycles, $40,000 for the salary of a teacher to support the math/ science labs, and a specific $3,750 grant to Riverton High School. Intel also provided a $110,000 grant to train 4,800 Utah teachers in computer use (Intel Corporation, 2004). The Gates Foundation has also offered grants to various states and organizations, focusing on the use of technology by school leaders (Bill & Melinda Gates Foundation, 2003). It offered $3.6 million to Virginia to create on-site training for principals and other administrators. It provided $4.2 million to Louisiana for a center for educational technology to support principals and administrators. And it gave $1 million to the International Society for Technology in Education and Educational Support Systems to create a think tank for users of educational technology.

Thus a huge sum of money has been offered by federal and state governments as well as the private sector to get technology into the classroom. The bulk of this financing has gone to hardware needs including purchasing computers and other multimedia equipment, wiring schools for the Internet and developing school networks, and wiring classrooms to one another and between schools. There have also been some investments in closing the digital divide in homes; laptop computers, community technology centers, and after-school computer labs all provide hardware access to students who do not have it in their homes. And increasingly, policymakers and business leaders have recognized that teachers are a weak link in using technology to promote student achievement. Many have called for or funded efforts to train teachers in computer use.

The issue, however, is much more complicated than increasing teachers' comfort with computers. While training may get teachers to use computers, it will not solve the other problem recognized by policymakers and business leaders: the need to integrate technology into the curriculum. Understanding technology is, at most, half the story of curriculum integration. The other half is understanding the curriculum and how instructional practices other than educational technology fit in. Only then can the proper place of technology be understood. Yet, the simultaneous movement for standards and assessments has called for generally improved teacher quality. Teachers, on average, lack an understanding of how to teach to higher academic standards, whether with computers or on blackboards. Only by understanding what needs to happen in improving teacher quality, can the weak link in the educational technology movement be addressed.

THE MOVEMENT TO IMPROVE TEACHER QUALITY

One response to *A Nation at Risk* was a growing interest in raising standards for teachers. Two reports in the late 1980s, the Carnegie report (Carnegie Forum on Education and the Economy, 1986) and the Holmes Group report (Holmes Group, Inc., 1986), pointed to the low quality of the teaching force and the need for reforms in the schools of education that prepare teachers and in the incentives provided to teachers as they progress through their careers. For example, the National Board on Professional Teaching Standards (NBPTS) was proposed by the Holmes Group to give teachers a route for career advancement other than leaving the classroom and becoming a principal.

Ten years later another report spawned various proposals for improvements in teacher quality. In *What Matters Most: Teaching for America's Future* (1996), the National Commission on Teaching and America's Future (NCTAF) declared that, without dramatic improvements in teacher quality, school systems would simply be unable to train students to meet the new academic standards. The report viewed the key problem as a failure of American society to treat teaching as a profession and recommended the following steps for professionalizing teaching:

1. *Link standards for teachers to standards for students.* Teachers are unlikely to be able to get students to meet standards they themselves cannot meet. States should establish professional boards of teaching standards, require that all schools of education be professionally accredited, license teachers based upon demonstrated performance, and use NBPTS standards as the benchmark for successful teaching.

2. *Reform preservice and in-service teacher training.* States, schools, and colleges should organize professional development around standards for students and teachers, increase the use of professional development schools (PDS) providing one-year graduate-level internships to prospective teachers, establish mentoring programs for new teachers, establish high-quality in-service training funded by a minimum of one percent of state and local spending, and embed the lessons of professional development in daily work.

3. *Improve teacher recruitment so that each classroom has a qualified teacher.* States should require that school districts hire only qualified teachers and give them sufficient funds

to do so, streamline hiring processes, make it easier for
teachers trained in one jurisdiction to work in another,
provide scholarships and loans to attract teachers in high-
needs subjects and locations, and investigate alternative
pathways for prospective teachers such as career changers
or paraprofessionals already in the classroom.

4. *Restructure school incentives to reward good teachers and
punish poor ones.* States should enact financial incentives for
teachers to meet NBPTS standards and remove incompetent
teachers.

5. *Reorganize schools to support effective teaching.* States and
localities should reallocate resources to provide more
for teachers and less for nonteaching personnel, recruit
principals whose focus is on instruction, and rethink
schedules to support in-depth learning.

The NCTAF report saw three national institutions as crucial
for driving school districts and schools of education toward higher
standards: the National Council for the Accreditation of Teacher
Education (NCATE), the Interstate New Teacher Assessment
and Support Consortium (INTASC), and the National Board
on Professional Teaching Standards (NBPTS). NCATE accredits
schools of education and increasingly seeks to align its standards
to national academic standards. INTASC assesses the credentials
of beginning teachers in the context of academic standards. And
NBPTS provides certification to advanced teachers, also consistent
with academic standards. These organizations could increase the
ability of teachers to teach to the new standards by increasing the
alignment of teacher and student standards. States could increase
the scope and influence of these organizations by requiring schools
of education to be accredited by NCATE, by requiring INTASC
assessments for permanent certification, and providing financial
incentives to teachers to go through certification by NBPTS.

Many of the changes envisaged by the NCTAF report have
indeed been taking place. More and more states now require NCATE
certification of schools of education (NCATE, 2003). More states
have become INTASC states, or have used some similar form of
beginning teacher assessment. And the number of NBPTS certified

teachers has grown exponentially over the last 5 years.

Federal, state, and local governments have also promulgated other policies not contemplated by NCTAF. At the federal level, the Clinton administration's primary emphasis had been on increasing the supply of teachers rather than its quality; its best known initiative in this area was the class size reduction initiative, which provided $4.6 billion in federal funds per year to assist school districts in bringing more teachers into the classroom. The Clinton administration also supported four programs for the professional development of teachers: the Eisenhower state grants ($485 million), the Eisenhower national program ($41 million), the Eisenhower federal program ($23 million), and the Eisenhower regional math and science education initiative ($15 million). As with technology, the key change under the Bush administration has been to consolidate these programs into a single block grant giving states flexibility as to how they allocate the money. Bush's teacher quality state grant was proposed at the $2.6 billion level in FY02, and incentives for those entering the teaching force at $30 million ("Final Fiscal," 2001). A great many additional ideas for improving teacher quality were tried by states and localities. New York State offered to finance the loans of students in state colleges who intended to go on to teach, while San Francisco offered subsidized housing for teachers. Many districts offered signing bonuses, and some, such as New York City, simply increased teacher salaries across the board. Some states responded to high numbers of uncertified teachers by setting certification deadlines; others stiffened certification requirements. Connecticut, for instance, requires teachers to have majored in the subject they are teaching.

Thus the movement to bring technology into the classroom comes amidst the larger concern regarding the fitness of many teachers to prepare students to meet high standards. The teacher problem, as it relates to technology, really has two parts. First, if teachers are not comfortable with technology, they will not be able to use it as an effective learning tool. Teachers often understand computers less well than their students, and are likely to respond either by not using computers at all or by using them in the simplest possible ways. Second, even if teachers are comfortable with technology, if they are not comfortable with the subject matter and pedagogy called for in their classroom, they will not be able to use computers effectively. If teachers don't understand the subject matter, they will not be able to select or evaluate digital content, or to help when students hit substantive hurdles. If teachers don't understand pedagogy, they will not have the background for placing technology among the range of pedagogical alternatives required to increase student learning, to say nothing of individualizing pedagogical techniques to the learning styles of particular students.

The ultimate inadequacy of teacher preparation, however, is not specific to technology. It lies in the neutrality of teacher standards. What is regarded as effective teaching, according to most standards, can be primarily didactic or primarily constructivist. For purposes of evaluating teacher quality, it is typically argued, teachers need to be assessed on their own terms. If their instructional goals are didactic, then they should be evaluated based upon their ability to apply didactic pedagogy. If their instructional goals are constructivist, a different rubric applies. For instance, in *Enhancing Professional Practice: A Framework for Teaching*, Charlotte Danielson (1996) acknowledges that her personal preference is for a constructivist approach to teaching. Her standards for evaluating effective teaching, however, are pedagogically neutral. In terms of classroom instruction, she calls for communicating clearly and accurately, using questioning and discussion techniques, engaging students in learning, providing feedback to students, and demonstrating flexibility and responsiveness. These components could just as easily be consistent with didactic pedagogy as with constructivist pedagogy.

What the rest of this book seeks to demonstrate is that technology must abandon its pedagogical neutrality. How technology is used is part and parcel of the overall instructional goals of the teacher and the academic standards they want their classes to meet. If these are inconsistent, the teacher will fail. If they are consistently didactic, students will be at a disadvantage. Only if standards, teaching, and technology are oriented in a constructivist fashion will students learn what they need to fully participate in the new economy—the economy of the era of high technology.

KEY POINTS

- The movements to raise academic standards, increase technology use, and improve teacher quality are all interrelated and all neutral on the subject of which pedagogy—didactic or constructivist—to use.
- The movement to raise academic standards culminated in No Child Left Behind, which requires schools and states to make adequate yearly progress in mathematics, science, and reading.
- The movement to increase technology use has been driven simultaneously by federal, state, and corporate programs, and has resulted in an average 5:1 ratio of students to computers in the classroom.
- Inadequacies in teacher quality are the primary obstacle to the effectiveness of educational technology; for teachers to use computers effectively they have to be taught both about using computers and about using the pedagogy most productive for computer use, namely constructivism.

CHAPTER 2

The Academic Debate: Supporters and Critics of Technology's Effectiveness

Researchers have been debating the effectiveness of computers as educational tools almost since their introduction. Computers first appeared in classrooms in the 1960s largely to provide students with opportunities to do exercises on their own that pertained to what teachers had covered in class. These computerized drill-and-practice activities, known as computer-assisted instruction (CAI), were the subject of hundreds of small-scale studies during the next 30 years. While the bulk of these studies found modest positive effects for the use of drill-and-practice computing, critiques of these studies have raised questions about the extent to which CAI helps, under what conditions it helps, and which students it helps.

During the 1980s and 1990s, the nature of the computer applications changed, but not the mixed nature of findings about their effectiveness. Apple Computers of Tomorrow (ACOT) was one of the most comprehensive attempts to move educational computing from drill-and-practice activities to more complex skills, known as higher order or critical-thinking skills. The impact of ACOT on various schools was evaluated, and while the results were often positive, the evaluators of ACOT raised questions about the ability of traditional experimental and quasi-experimental studies to capture the impact of ACOT on teaching and learning. Outright critics of technology, such as Larry Cuban, went further, arguing that there was no evidence at all of technology's effectiveness, but a great deal of evidence to the contrary. Later in this chapter I will examine the positive effects of technology identified by the ACOT program, the questions raised by its evaluators, and the critique of technology presented by Larry Cuban (1986, 2001) in his historical work on technology as well as his own study of the use of technology in classrooms in the heart of Silicon Valley. But first, it is important to summarize the results of the studies of the more primitive form of educational technology, the drill-and-practice approach known as computer-assisted instruction.

THE RECORD ON CAI

The nature of CAI studies has required summaries of their results to take the form of meta-analyses, which aggregate the results from numerous small-scale studies of a given topic. Beginning with the Suppes and Morningstar study (1968), these studies have tended to be small in scale, consisting of a few schools or classrooms. Suppes and Morningstar compared the Stanford Achievement Test scores of 925 CAI students with those of 1,025 students receiving traditional instruction. The results of such studies were combined through meta-analyses using statistics to determine the average effect of the CAI intervention on student outcomes. The meta-analyses generally found modest positive effects for CAI (Kulik, Bangert-Drowns, & Williams, 1983; Kulik & Kulik, 1991; Kulik, Kulik, & Cohen, 1980; Niemiec & Walberg, 1989).

The meta-analyses, however, also examined the conditions under which CAI had positive, negative, or no effects, and found a great deal of variation. Burns and Bozeman (1981), for example, found positive effects for high- and low-performing students, but not for medium-level ones. Baird and Koballa (1986) found positive effects when CAI was used as part of certain pedagogies, but not others. Driscoll (1990) found that the effectiveness of CAI depended upon student learning styles, and Clark (1984) found that effectiveness depended upon students' beliefs about computers. Others found that effectiveness depended upon the digital content employed and the level of teacher training (Dence, 1980; Forman, 1982).

The study of Niemiec, Samson, Weinstein, and Walberg (1987) illustrates the degree to which positive effects are dependent upon the circumstances of the intervention and the study of it. They meta-analyzed 48 studies. On average they found that students exposed to CAI scored in the 65th percentile when comparable students not exposed to CAI were in the 50th percentile. They then examined the impact of 45 variables on this benefit of CAI. They found that the effect varied by:

- *Publication type.* Dissertations showed smaller effects than articles.
- *Student achievement.* Students at higher levels of achievement gained less.
- *Cognitive complexity of the task.* More complex tasks meant smaller gains.
- *Duration of implementation.* Longer duration meant smaller gains.

Other meta-analyses showed similar patterns. Liao (1992) examined 31 studies and found three-fourths showed positive effects. The effect depended upon the kind of statistics reported, the type of computer used, and the duration of the intervention. More recently, Christmann, Badgett, and Lucking (1997) examined CAI studies over the course of the previous 12 years. While they too found a modest positive effect (the 57th percentile compared to the 50th for non-CAI students), they found that the size of the effect decreased markedly over the period under study (the 1980s and 1990s).

Critiques of the CAI studies have pointed to various methodological problems that could explain the instability of the results (Colorado, 1988). CAI research varied in the organization and clarity of its reports, the use of methods that might reduce study validity (Babbie, 2002), and the confusion between the effects of computers and the effects of instruction—namely, that better teachers were more likely to try innovative techniques such as CAI, but students of such teachers would likely have benefited from innovation whether it was channeled through CAI or some other instructional technique.

Studies that introduce cost into their design have raised questions about the cost-effectiveness of CAI. Levin, Glass, and Meister (1987), for instance, found that while implementing CAI was a more cost-effective way to improve student achievement than making classes smaller, it was less cost-effective than tutoring.

In sum, then, the picture provided by the CAI studies of the 1960s, 1970s, and 1980s is a murky one; CAI holds some promise, but results seem highly dependent upon methodology.

THE ACOT EXPERIENCE

During the 1980s, Apple Computers introduced a very different kind of intervention into the classroom. CAI was, for the most part, a set of drill-and-practice activities that students undertook individually, without much interaction with teachers or other students. When students were not on computers, the balance of time was typically spent on "direct instruction," meaning lectures and some discussion between the teacher and the class as a whole. ACOT sought to change the role of computers in the classroom and, in so doing, also change the interactions between students and teachers and among students. Rather than involving drill and practice, ACOT focused on student-initiated work, long-term projects, access to multiple learning resources, and small group work.

The notion was that such computer-based activities would change teaching in five stages (Sandholtz, Ringstaff, & Dwyer, 1997). First, in the *entry stage*, teachers would act like first-year teachers, focused on crises stemming from technical glitches, with a concomitant lack of time to address them. Second, in the *adoption stage*, teachers would try to fit computers into a direct instruction approach to teaching students how to use computers for keyboarding and word processing. Third, in the *adaptation stage*, teachers would use computers to teach basic skills, and when they discovered that students could get through the material more quickly than expected, teachers would begin to teach problem-solving techniques. Fourth, in the *appropriation stage*, computers would become a necessity for teachers; they would perceive computers as a vital instructional tool. Finally, in the *invention stage*, teachers would move from direct instruction to student-centered, collaborative, project-based learning.

Researchers found that this model of teacher practice did in fact play out in the ACOT schools. The adaptation stage, for instance, occurred in both mathematics and language arts in sixth-grade classrooms. In math, the stage began with teachers devoting 30–

40% of their time to CAI-like basic-skills uses of computers. The students managed to finish the material early, and teachers used the balance of the time to teach higher order thinking skills. In language arts, teachers found that students wrote more quickly on computers and could go through more drafts more easily. In the invention stage, students put together a model city in social studies and developed their own calculators in math. Findings from a study of five school sites around the country included a shift in teaching practice toward more group work and less lecturing, as well as greater focus on higher order thinking skills.

Despite ACOT's success in changing teacher practice, evaluators of ACOT were not able to capture effects on student performance. While students did not lose ground in vocabulary, reading comprehension, and math concepts compared to peers not exposed to ACOT, neither did they make gains. The evaluators of ACOT attributed these findings to the difficulty of properly evaluating such programs. In the first place, the tests were not geared toward the kinds of skills ACOT was seeking to convey, rather, the tests involved basic skills whereas ACOT was seeking to convey higher order thinking skills. Second, the programs, both the ACOT ones and those to which they were compared, changed a great deal over time. In particular, teachers used ACOT differently in some stages than others, and it was difficult for the assessment used by evaluators to keep up with these changes. Indeed, the fact that teachers were experimenting with computers meant that the nature of the intervention changed over time. Finally, there were many side effects to the introduction of ACOT that might have affected outcomes. Not only did the ACOT classrooms not stand still, neither did the schools. ACOT principals, seeking change, did not limit themselves to ACOT, and non-ACOT principals often pursued changes of their own. Thus the evaluators questioned whether proper conclusions about ACOT could be drawn one way or the other (Baker, Gearhart, & Herman, 1993).

LARRY CUBAN ON EDUCATIONAL TECHNOLOGY

One researcher was not particularly surprised by the ambiguous findings on ACOT. Larry Cuban, an expert on educational history, had studied how, time and time again, some fad or another had been introduced into schools only to be replaced by another fad before it made any difference. And the fads that lasted seemed to be things that teachers had been doing in the first place anyway. He thus came to the study of computers with the notion that the effectiveness of any intervention would rise and fall with the ability and interest of teachers to make use of it; if it did not help them get through the day, the innovation would end up in the trash can.

Cuban first tackled these issues in his 1986 history of educational technology, *Teachers and Machines: The Classroom Use of Technology Since 1920*. He defined educational technology broadly, including not just computers but whatever tools teachers used to help instruct students. Thus in the nineteenth century, the predominant technologies were chalk, blackboards, writing tablets, and McGuffey readers. In the twentieth century, school administrators sought to introduce a whole new set of technologies that, in retrospect, sound ridiculous, but at the time were accompanied by the same rhetoric that computers receive today: that they would change the nature of instruction, dramatically increasing student performance. First came the use of reel-to-reel films in the classroom. Then radios and televisions made their way into the classroom. There was even an experiment to teach children from airplanes—talk about experiential learning! In all of these cases, the innovation tended to get shelved because the amount of trouble involved in using the technology was not worth the teacher's time and effort. Teachers, in Cuban's view, were largely resistant to technological change, with only the most innovative teachers (the techno-enthusiasts) and the least innovative teachers (who use filmstrips to kill time) making use of it.

When Cuban wrote his history, the experiences of ACOT had not come to light. Most technology was still of the CAI type. But in light of the experience of the late 1980s and early 1990s, Cuban decided to undertake his own study of precisely how teachers were using computers in one of the most technology-rich environments in the country, Silicon Valley. Building on the work of ACOT scholars Sandholz, Ringstaff, and Dwyer (1997), Cuban sought to discover where teachers in technology-rich classrooms lay on the continuum of stages. He decided to focus on students of three age levels—preschool-kindergarten, high school, and college. He chose preschool because of the concerns expressed by many educators and organizations of educators of young children that computers might not be developmentally appropriate for them, and he chose high school because of its significance for preparing students for college and the workforce. He chose college because of its organizational distinctiveness from K–12 settings, but that part of the study is outside the scope of this book.

At the preschool level, Cuban looked at 11 classrooms. First, he found that most of these classrooms lacked sufficient computers for educational technology to be used in the innovative ways suggested by ACOT and other advocates of using computers for advanced skills. Given that classrooms are generally seen as technology rich when they have at least one computer for every five students, only 3 of the classrooms were adequately infused with technology. Cuban then looked at the ways in which teachers used computers in preschool and found most teachers to be arrested in the adoption stage, meaning that they were using their computers to support the teaching of basic skills and had not successfully integrated them into the curriculum.

In high school, the findings differed somewhat. In terms of student access to computers, the two high schools he studied did indeed prove to have technology rich environments. Flatland High School had a student to computer ratio of 5:1, and Las Montanas High School, a ratio of 4:1. Teachers also seemed to be integrating computers into their curricula, at least when Cuban asked them. Out of the 21 teachers he interviewed, Cuban found that 60% reported that the availability of technology had significantly improved their teaching techniques. But when Cuban actually shadowed the teachers, watching what they did in the classroom, he found that most of the teachers were still using more traditional, basic skills–oriented practices.

> All but a few of the 35 teachers (in both schools) used a familiar repertoire of instructional approaches. These routinely lectured, orchestrated a group discussion, reviewed homework, worked on assignments and occasionally used overhead projectors and videos. (Cuban, 2001, p. 95)

Although computers were available, teachers were not using them; and when they did, it was at an adoption stage of use, reinforcing basic skills. Thus, as Cuban had concluded in his 1986 history book, teachers tended not to embrace the new technology.

Significant shortcomings to Cuban's study (2001) and thus to his conclusions need to be noted, however. The numbers of schools, teachers, and students he chose were relatively small. He examined only 11 preschool classrooms and 2 high schools. At the high school level, he talked to only 21 teachers. Not only were the numbers small, but it is unlikely that they are representative of schools, students, and teachers in the nation as a whole. His schools were limited to the Silicon Valley area, which is more technology savvy than most areas; indeed, many of these students had parents who worked for the technology companies. The students also tend to be more affluent than the typical student in the United States. Only by collecting data from large numbers of schools, teachers, and students that are representative of the nation as a whole is it possible to draw conclusions for the nation as a whole about how much access there is to technology, how it is used, and whether it has an impact on student performance. Unfortunately, most of the studies done around the time of Cuban's have largely the same shortcomings as Cuban's. For instance, one study found positive benefits—though extremely small—to technology, but was limited in scope to schools in West Virginia (Mann, Shakeshaft, Becker, & Kottkamp, 1999). The current study seeks, for the first time, to use a national sample of students, teachers, and schools to relate access to and use of technology to student performance.

KEY POINTS

- Early research on the effectiveness of educational technology examined computer-assisted instruction, in which technology is used to support drill-and-practice activities. The findings of these studies proved inconsistent.
- Apple Computers of Tomorrow used technology to try to make instruction more oriented toward higher order thinking skills, and evaluators found that teaching practices did indeed change. The evidence on the impact on student achievement, however, proved mixed.

- Critics of educational technology, such as Larry Cuban, suggest that teachers generally resist changing their instructional techniques and computers are unlikely to leverage such changes. While there is significant historical basis for this point of view, Cuban's evidence applying this point of view to current technology uses, such as ACOT, is fairly weak.

CHAPTER 3

Tales of Educational Technology

With its enormous investments in educational technology, the United States is full of examples of effective and ineffective uses. The various diatribes against educational technology happily point to examples of its failure: classrooms where students are in disarray, computers are malfunctioning, and teachers are helpless. All of this money, the critics say, was spent for toys that nobody can use. Supporters of technology counter with utopian visions of classrooms where two or three students are huddled around each computer, watching attentively as one of their number plots three-dimensional graphs from data on the Web on economics, demographics, or global warming. These effective and ineffective uses, however, are not random events; they are part of a pattern. Depending upon the quality of instruction teachers are offering, the technology will be used or misused. If a teacher cannot manage the class, the students will not work well with computers. And the key determinant of instructional quality is whether it conforms to a didactic or constructivist model; anecdotes of computer disasters tend to occur in didactic environments, and anecdotes of technological success in constructivist environments.

There are many anecdotes in the literature to support each model, but I'll add some of my own to the mix. Before telling my stories, however, I think it is important to tell someone else's very old story. It is so old, in fact, that there are no computers in it. But technology is in evidence, and the theme is the same as this book's, that a combination of good teachers and good media can allow students to think very abstractly and become good problem solvers.

THE *MENO*

The story I wish to tell is how Socrates, an Athenian philosopher in the late fifth-century B.C., taught a slave how to understand square roots. The story—the *Meno*—comes from Plato, one of Socrates' students, so whether it is fact or fiction, only Plato could tell. It takes the form of a dialogue between Socrates and the slave, with the slave's owner, Meno, interjecting on occasion. Imagine it as occurring outdoors, in an area surrounded by classical Greek buildings with their magisterial stairways and marble roofs supported by tall white columns. The characters are sitting on the ground, where they can draw geometrical sketches with sticks in the dirt—a decidedly low-tech operation. Socrates wants to demonstrate that all people, from the most miserable slave to the most powerful king, have knowledge within them of which they are not aware until their teachers help them draw it out. He does so by choosing a young slave, whom Meno admits has little, if any, education, and teaching him how to figure out what amounts to the geometrical equivalent of a square root—if the area of a square is known, what is the length of its sides? The Greeks generally developed mathematical concepts geometrically; they were relatively ignorant of algebra.

Socrates does two things: draws shapes and asks questions. All further information comes from the boy. First, Socrates draws a square. Since it is a square, the boy holds that all four sides (AB, BC, CD, and AD) are equal, and that the lines that bisect it (EF and GH) are also equal. The boy then indicates that the rectangle of one half of the square would have an area of 2 feet, and that therefore the full square would have an area of 4 feet. Then Socrates asks the boy to draw a square with an area of 8 feet, and tell him the length of each side, to which the boy answers 4 feet. Socrates then draws a more complicated square, in which the length of the sides has been doubled from two to four, and in this case the boy acknowledges that the area would be 16 feet. Then the boy argues that if the desired area is between 4 and 16 feet, the length must be between 2 and 4 feet, namely 3 feet. But that leads to an area of 9 feet. "Then what length will we give it [the side of the square]? Try to tell us exactly. If you don't want to count it up, just show us on the diagram." The boy responds in perplexity, "It's no use Socrates, I just don't know"

(Hamilton & Kairns, 1987, p. 368). At this point, Socrates notes that the boy has made intellectual progress, from thinking he knew the side of a square to be 8 feet, to realizing he did not. Socrates then points out the consequence of this discovery of ignorance. "In fact, we have helped him to some extent toward finding out the right answer for now not only is he ignorant of it, but he will be quite glad to look for it" (p. 369). The boy is now highly motivated. Socrates turns toward the solution, again using geometry. He coaches the child into drawing a figure like the one where BD, DH, BE, and EH are diagonals in their squares. The boy then determines that the area of AFGJ is 16 feet and that BDHE is half that area. Thus BD is the length of a side of a square which has an area of 8 feet.

This example is useful for many reasons, and has frequently been a topic of discussion among educational philosophers. For our purposes, however, it illustrates the essence of constructivist pedagogy and its relationship to technology. First it can be seen that the lesson conforms to the principles of constructivism discussed at the beginning of the book. It introduces an abstraction—the square root—and then derives its calculation from concrete models. Indeed, the problem is set up so that the student finds out what he does not know and concludes with him realizing how he can figure it out (by calculating the length of a hypotenuse). The lesson is also highly individualized. Socrates makes sure that all positive information comes from the student, and Socrates chooses his course of action based upon what the student knows and does not know. Assessment is completely unobtrusive, built into the lesson. Socrates anticipates that at some point the student will admit his ignorance and at some point he will know the answer. In the meantime, because the boy has to respond to the questioning, Socrates is continually testing the student's engagement in the process. The extent to which the class is teacher or student directed is more complex. While the student provides all the answers, Socrates does ask him many leading questions. Thus, while the student constructs the knowledge, he does so under Socrates' direction. Questioning, depending upon its obtrusiveness, can make a teacher more of a sage or more of a guide. But, as discussed earlier, this is not the key constructivist distinction.

Ultimately, what Socrates provides is not questions, but technology. His technology is very basic. He and the student draw figures in the dirt with a stick. But this visualization of the concept Socrates is introducing is what makes it possible for the student to construct his own knowledge. Without the geometrical figures, the student would be forced to do straight arithmetic in his head, and this might be too complex for him to keep straight. Geometry, as Kant has taught us, is the technology that makes abstract mathematical concepts real; a square is just as real as a tree, and can be directly experienced simply by drawing it.

In a constructivist classroom, then, we have the teacher, the medium, and the student. The virtue of the medium is that it facilitates the understanding of the student, turning a concept into a concrete problem that it is within the student's grasp to answer. Before describing some contemporary classrooms that use computers and the Internet successfully, in a constructivist fashion, I think it may be worthwhile to describe a contemporary classroom that uses technology unsuccessfully, in a didactic fashion.

A COMPUTER LAB IN URBAN HIGH SCHOOL, USA

Urban High School is a comprehensive neighborhood high school with more than 2,000 students. Nearly all of the students are African American or Latino and qualify for reduced-price or free lunches. Built in the 1970s, the campus consists of a round central building and two attached wings. Students enter the building through one of many doors lined up in the front of the central building. Here they go through metal detectors, and those who set them off are searched with handheld scanners. In the mornings students tend to congregate in front of the doors as they wait to go through security. Many arrive without any learning materials whatsoever—not only no textbooks, but no pens or paper. Once through security, students go upstairs to the second, third, or fourth floors; the first floor is for administrative offices. The wings of the school house student lockers and some classrooms. Because the wings are separated from the main area by doors, they are excellent places for students who do not have classes or who are cutting classes to spend time with their friends. Students also feel free to walk around and around the main building, which is circular. The floor is covered with trash, which students occasionally put in wastebaskets and set on fire. The principal of the school is rarely seen outside of his office on the first floor; the office is an island of calm and tranquility in a sea of loitering, vandalism, and violence. There are large numbers of security guards who, after finishing checking students as they come into the building, do regular "sweeps" of the main building, in which they go around the circle to pick up students who should be in class and send them to detention. Naturally, these students are replaced by a new set, so the corridors have to be swept frequently during the day.

Because most students prefer to be in the hallways with their friends, the classroom itself is a place of relative safety. One such room is the computer lab, consisting of about 20 PCs networked to one another, a teacher's PC, and the Web. Since many students do not go to class, there are more computers than students. As I enter the classroom with the students, I find the teacher sitting at her desk. She tells me to take a seat anywhere I like, and tells the students to go to their computers and get to work. Since these are the good students, they dutifully go to their computers, boot them up, and log on. They then click on an icon for a math program I won't do the service of advertising, although many readers may recognize it from my description. The screen displays a simple algebraic equation. Students then type in any numbers they want to divide the equation by or subtract from both sides. They continue to do these manipulations until they solve for x (at most, in three steps). They then go on to a number of similar problems. After about a half hour of this, not surprisingly, some of the students get bored. One brings up solitaire and begins to play. Another powers down his computer and begins writing something on a notepad: "Got to get this ready for my next class," he tells me when I look at him inquiringly. "Quiet down!" says the teacher, all but invisible behind her desk and its computer. The student shakes his neighbor's hand and smiles at me. Soon after, the bell sounds, and class is dismissed.

It would be foolish to place all of the blame for the lack of learning that occurred in that classroom on the didactic nature of the software. Many phenomena occurred at the same time to create this "perfect storm" of mindlessness. The overall school environment, for one, signaled to the students in that classroom that learning was not valued. As I have found again and again in my observations of urban schools with serious discipline problems and in a national study I conducted a few years ago about school discipline (Barton, Coley, & Wenglinsky, 1998), school disorder makes learning extremely difficult, if not impossible. Add to that a lack of educational leadership and a teacher indifferent to what her students are doing in class beyond keeping quiet, and it is hard to blame the technology. This is why it seems terribly unfair when books by technology's critics write off technology, providing one anecdote after another of students failing to learn in technology-rich environments when those students are being confronted with all of the conditions of a failing school: lack of discipline, invisible leadership, and ineffective teaching. Even the greatest software would not work under such conditions. All of that said, the nature of the medium is a part of the problem. A series of self-contained drills does not so much replace the teacher as allow the teacher to replace herself. The mindlessness of the drills bores the students, making them leave class less motivated than when they entered— and these were the most motivated students to begin with. But there are other schools with similar technology, which is put to more effective use.

CO-NECT AND THE ALL SCHOOL

Very often, technology's critics find failing schools and blame the technology. But at other times, they look successful schools in the face and label them failures. Such has been the fate of the Accelerated Learning Laboratory, a high school in Worcester, Massachusetts, the flagship school of a network of schools referred to as Co-nect. Todd Oppenheimer (2003), in *The Flickering Mind*, describes his visit to the ALL school, as it is known, and decried the learning taking place as superficial. To prove his point, he noted that one student prepared a PowerPoint presentation in civics class that had "clean graphics" and "digestible writing" but that it was no "deeper" than work one sees done with pencil and paper by seventh and eighth graders. In that same class, he claimed, many of the students did not know answers to a question about "the purpose and powers of Congress." From this one class, he concluded that the ALL school, like most that use technology, is an "unthinking trend follower" and not a "real school."

Co-nect began as part of the New American Schools Development Corporation initiative (NAS). The idea behind NAS was to fund various programs that created a design for an effective school and then provide technical assistance to schools across the country to implement the designs (Berends, Bodilly, & Kirby, 2002). The theory of change behind NAS was that schools could not improve on their own; rather, change had to be leveraged through a collaboration between the school and an external program that had a vision for how to improve the school. NAS sent out a request for proposals in 1989 and eight designs were ultimately funded. Co-nect distinguished itself in two interrelated ways. First, it was the design that focused the most on technology. While it had other components of a largely constructivist nature, such as an emphasis on students working on extended projects, it required schools to invest heavily in technology. Consequently, it had the start-up costs estimated in one study at $588 per student as opposed to a more typical cost for a NAS design of about $200 (American Institutes for Research, 1999). It was thus a relatively expensive constructivist approach to using technology. In 1994, Congress passed the Obey-Porter Act to reauthorize the Elementary and Secondary Education Act. The reauthorization provided for federal dollars to go to schools that adopted comprehensive school reform designs, meaning the NAS designs or other programs with similar theories of action that had been added to the Obey-Porter list. Over the years, despite its high start-up costs, Co-nect has attracted 80 schools from across the country. The first of these was ALL, and because it takes a relatively long time for schools to implement the designs, I thought it only fair to visit the oldest one. What I found was the complete opposite of what Oppenheimer described. Not only did ALL prove to be an effective school where deep learning was taking place, but it helped me reconceptualize the proper role of technology in the school.

The day I went to visit ALL I drove to Worcester from Boston. Normally this would not be a problem, but it was February, and the area was experiencing its worst blizzard in 5 years. So I had plenty of time, slogging down the unplowed highway, to think about what I wanted to ask about the school. Since I knew my focus was on technology, I figured I'd ask teachers and students to show me every way in which technology is being used. So I soldiered on to

Worcester, and as the snow continued to fall, I worried that I was on a wild-goose chase. Not to worry, it was business as usual, with two anchor-students giving the morning news report to homerooms on closed circuit TV as I arrived. The building consisted of a couple of stories, extremely tidy and well kept up. Students could not be in the hallway for long without a teacher asking them where they belonged. I began my meeting with the principal by asking her to tell me about the technology in the school. "Let me tell you about our program first," she responded. She went on to describe how students worked in groups on various projects. The projects could be anything from the ecology of Antarctica (appropriately enough) to the sociology of San Francisco. Students were not assessed by tests, but by collections of their project results. Students were expected to do a great deal of writing for their projects. The projects were to be as tied into real-world phenomena as possible while illustrating general concepts of the discipline—biology, chemistry, and so on. "But what about the technology?" I asked. "Well, in mathematics," the principal said, "you should probably talk to the math teacher, because math is more structured than the other subjects. In terms of the other subjects, because everything is a project, very often students use technology. And they are asked to make their final products available on the school's network. Why don't you look at what the students have up?"

So I did, and the projects were extremely sophisticated. I hate to disagree with Mr. Oppenheimer, but my own view is that the quality of work was, with a few exceptions, the kind of work you see in an advanced placement course. There was indeed a project on the ecology of Antarctica, with daily measurements of temperature, snowfall, wind velocity, and detailed research into the ever-widening ozone hole. The technology included downloads from relevant Web sites, chat rooms with oceanographers and naturalists, spreadsheets of data collected and analyzed, and slideshows using, yes, PowerPoint to present pictures of the snowscapes.

I also took up the principal's invitation to speak with the math teacher. We talked in the math room. "There are so few computers," I said, "not enough for every student. How can you make use of the technology?" She responded that the technology was just a tool, albeit a very helpful one. The curriculum she was teaching was called Integrated Math, where the level of difficulty progresses over the years but in any given year includes algebra, geometry, and trigonometry. "We have to be a little more traditional and use textbooks because there is a lot of material to cover." But the focus, she said, was not on breadth of coverage, but depth. "I would rather have the students spend an entire period on one problem, coming up with multiple ways of solving it, many of them dead-ends, than have them solve 15 problems without engaging their brains." In other words, she taught students to be active problem solvers. "But what about the technology?" I asked again. She replied that, right now, she had them develop templates in Lotus to use for algebra and graphing. But she'd been looking for more sophisticated software to manipulate equations and do matrix algebra in the more advanced classes.

At the end of the day, I went back to the principal. I was working at Educational Testing Service at the time, and she said to me, "So you're a testing person. Explain to me why the scores of my students on the state standardized tests are so mediocre." Apparently, parents are very impressed when they see their students' portfolios (as I had been), but get upset when their children end up around the mean on the tests. Obviously, there are two possible reasons for the discrepancy. Either the school is doing a poor job, or the tests are. Despite being a "testing person," I would have to say that the problem in this case was with the tests.

Like computers, tests are only a tool. There are good tests and bad tests, and appropriate uses for tests and inappropriate uses for tests. Most standardized state tests rely chiefly on multiple choice questions to measure whether students have acquired basic skills or absorbed certain knowledge. Only the best standardized tests include questions, like essays, that more closely resemble what students do in the classroom because so-called extended-response items are expensive to develop, administer, and grade. And only the best standardized tests measure student acquisition of higher order thinking skills and advanced concepts. If you want to imagine a good standardized test, think of an Advanced Placement Test, or the NAEP, which we will use frequently in the next chapter. When a school is constructivist and the test is the typical state standardized test, the school will be at a disadvantage. While the students taking the test will be more sophisticated in the subject than the average student—and this should give them an edge—they will also be less used to thinking in the mechanical way called for by the basic skills nature of the material and the multiple choice format of the test. Remember, ALL was not assessing students with tests aside from the state-mandated ones. And constructivist schools like ALL tend not to "teach to the test" or do "test prep" as many other schools do to boost their scores. Thus, with a basic skills state test, the constructivist approach proves a wash.

I think I left ALL learning more from them than they did from me. The lesson they learned from the "test guy" was that there were only two ways to fix their problem: change the curriculum by abandoning constructivism, or get the state to improve the sensitivity of the test to constructivist skills, a singularly unlikely prospect. The key lesson for me was that technology cannot stand alone. In successful technology-rich schools, technology is part of the culture and is inseparable from creative teaching, engaged students, and active leadership, all of which I saw in abundance at ALL. Oppenheimer left ALL thinking that the teachers and students talked about technology too much. I left the school realizing that it was I who was talking about technology too much.

TWO EXPEDITIONARY LEARNING SCHOOLS

Expeditionary Learning–Outward Bound (EL) was another of the NAS designs that received subsequent support from the Obey-Porter Act. The focus of EL is on organizing curricula into "learning expeditions." Such expeditions are analogous to what Outward Bound did for years before it developed the EL design, namely, take young people on physically and emotionally challenging expeditions to wilderness areas. In the context of schools, some of these expeditions continued to be literal, involving hiking, rappelling, or rafting, but others were figurative expeditions, such as learning how a newspaper works or how a trial is conducted. Many of the schools discovered that a good way to get students the experience of an expedition without requiring them to leave the classroom was to have a virtual expedition, in which their projects used technology.

A good example of a school that developed literal and virtual expeditions in tandem is the Roots and Wings Community Schools

(RWCS), forty miles north of Taos, New Mexico. The area is extremely rural, consisting of farms, wilderness, and mountains. Taos itself is an artistic community that has been around for nearly a century. The galleries there contain works of art that draw their inspiration from the beautiful setting of the surrounding mountains. The school is a small charter school, which, as shall be seen, also draws its inspiration from its setting. Its being a charter school means that it is exempt from many state mandates surrounding public schools, but is still a public school. And when I say the school is small, I mean it. It is run by two couples and has 21 students in sixth through eighth grade. The students are generally ones who had difficulty in a more traditional school setting. The two couples live right across the street from the school in two small wood houses.

In its most recent academic year, the school focused on the theme of the Age of Exploration. It consisted of work done with computers in the classroom and an extended field trip that was ultimately documented on computer. The work done in the classroom involved learning about a series of explorers. Students were each assigned an explorer, about whom they had to collect information from the Web and from books. These explorers included non-Europeans and Europeans who did not go to the New World, such as Marco Polo, but the focus was on how the explorers were largely an extension of the European Renaissance. (The Renaissance was studied as part of another project in which students did research on a particular aspect of the Renaissance.) Students also learned about the explorers' destinations. Each student researched a country in Africa, South America, Central America, and the Caribbean. Students wrote a historical time line about the place, as well as descriptions of the climate, terrain, and some statistic of interest such as a demographic. All of these reports (on the explorers and the places) were uploaded to the Web.

The literal expedition made what had been learned in the virtual expeditions concrete. The school went on a 10-day 25-mile rafting trip down the San Juan River in southeastern Utah. The trip was christened by two patrons, named King Budinand and Queen Nancybella. During the expedition, the students kept journals, collected data on flora (e.g., tamarisk, fleabane) and fauna (e.g., geese, herons, big-horn sheep), constructed star charts, and examined petroglyphs, pictographs from an ancient Native

American people, the Anasazi. The write-ups were organized scientifically with introductions, methods, results, and conclusions, and after the expedition these were uploaded to the Web.

What the RWCS demonstrated to me was the essential interchangeability of media. To be sure, educational technology and whitewater rafting had their distinctive characteristics, with respective strengths and weaknesses. For instance, it would be harder to have done whitewater rafting if the school were located in New York City, and there certainly would not have been petroglyphs available. The trips also require 24-hour commitments among students and teachers, making it difficult to do them year round. On the other hand, virtual reality is just that—virtual. It mimics reality, but is not itself reality, and consequently the experience is somewhat less "real-world." But these distinctive characteristics aside, what both have in common is that they are media that are particularly well suited to constructivist pedagogy. Both use the key idea of constructivism, making abstractions concrete through problem solving. The notion of exploration was made historically and geographically concrete through an actual voyage. Because of the project-based structure, students were able to initiate their own projects and work at their own pace. As might be expected with a single class that mixed sixth, seventh, and eighth graders, the quality of the projects was heterogeneous. Both virtual and real expeditions also lent themselves to collaborative forms of learning. For the trip, students were organized into teams. In the classroom, time was built in for self-reflection and peer critiques of work. And assessment was primarily the work uploaded to the Web.

Another EL middle school, this one in Portland, Maine, raised for me the question of the line between what is technology and what isn't. King Middle School is a two-story building. The students are divided into two "houses"—Windsor and York. The students are fairly diverse demographically. Sixty percent qualify for free or reduced-price lunches, 70% come from single-parent families, and 22% are foreign born, coming from 18 different countries. The school includes an outdoor component, as would be expected at Outward Bound. Students attend Camp King in September, where they hike, do sports and theater, and experience a one-hour "solo," where they are alone at a wilderness site. For the rest of the year, students do various projects at the school. Some of the ones I saw were

"Voices of the United States," in which students visit businesses in Portland and talk to owners about their experiences as immigrants; a study of the intertidal zone in a cove off of the Atlantic Ocean; and testing various cleaners for how good they are at resisting bacteria, using petri dishes and incubators (that learning expedition was appropriately entitled "Yuck!"). All project results were uploaded to the Web.

My particular favorite was a project called "Fading Footprints." Each student was given a laptop. They then chose an animal that was endangered and used the laptop to check the Web for information. All of the individual projects were brought together to produce a CD. Other components of the project included drawing the animal by finding its picture, making a grid, and filling in each box in the grid based upon the original picture. The drawings were then scanned onto the students' Web page. Students also had to write concept papers on issues around the endangerment of the species and critique the work of their peers. Other activities included fieldwork, such as raising salmon eggs, doing scientific classifications, writing a natural history of the animal, writing a physical description, a personal essay, and a bibliography. An example of an essay illustrates how successfully this project got students to state an abstract proposition and then illustrate it.

> [The concept:] Diversity strengthens an ecosystem because if there isn't a wide enough selection of organisms in an ecosystem, then the different species have to change their main food source, which might cause an imbalance in the food chain.

> [The concrete:] For example, if for some crazy reason all the plankton in the ocean were to go extinct, then some of the fishes' main food source would be depleted so they would most likely become endangered and maybe go extinct. So if all of the fish in the sea were to die, then many of the seabirds would be in serious trouble, and maybe go extinct. Then the predators that prey on the seabirds would eventually die without their main food supply. So, as you can see, if the smallest of all organisms were to die, most of the world's ecosystem could be destroyed. If we have more species in the

food chain, the stronger the ecosystem is. But if an animal has to rely on a different food source for a while or forever, then the diversity in the ecosystem can help because it gives the animal something else to eat.

I also quite liked the medieval and earthquake projects. The medieval project had the York and Windsor houses doing two separate things. The Windsor house did a set of skits about the middle ages. It was heavily research based, involving reading medieval literature, researching a particular century (the fourteenth), and doing a timeline. York house built a medieval city, by researching medieval architecture. The students had to be able to explain the functions of the different parts of the city. For instance, the moat deterred people from entering the city, not only because they would need to swim across, but also because it contained the collective excrement of the castle and so would be unpleasant and make the interloper sick. In the earthquake project, students built various structures that were then subjected to a vigorous shaking to see if they would stand. A similar project with sailboats had students build them and then have them float down a tank while being subjected to the winds of a fan. This latter project made clear that poor boat construction could be deadly.

The question these activities raise is not where is the technology, but where isn't it. Computers are used to some degree for all the projects. Project results are uploaded, and CDs are made that summarize each project. The CDs generally include project data as well as movies made with videocameras of some of the classroom activities. Having students work under a lens, so many of them said, forces them to reflect on what they are doing as they are doing it, to say nothing of the reflection involved at the end of the project in clipping the video and producing the CD. Also, because of the Maine laptop initiative, students had access to laptops that had wireless connections to the Internet, making their research much easier—many could go at it 24/7. But technology use was hardly limited to computers and CDs. Designing a boat that can catch the wind in its sails and move straight is a project involving questions of technology. Designing earthquake resistant towers involves thinking about architectural concepts and applying to them a technology that predates computers. And building a castle (as well as projectile weapons to attack it) involves thinking about how to work within the confines of the technology of an earlier age. To some extent, then, all project-based learning involves a technological medium. What makes it constructivist is that the technology creates a series of problems to be solved that illustrate the underlying concept to be conveyed. Thus students learn the concept by doing, internalizing it rather than letting it bounce off their armor, figuratively speaking.

HIGH TECH HIGH

One important philosophy of education, consistent with, if not a key piece of, the constructivist approach, is the notion that all learning has to be closely tied to its practical uses. As Rousseau (2003) tells us in *Emile*, his chronicle of the education of a hypothetical student, children will be most motivated to learn when they can see a connection between the concept and some practical need in their life such as making a living or crossing a river. The view of business leaders on what constitutes an effective education goes along the same lines. In this new technological age, employers want workers who can think independently and solve complex problems. As the watershed report of business leaders, Society's Commission on Achieving Necessary Skills (1992), makes clear, the only way schools can accomplish this is by emphasizing higher order thinking skills. The students who will get the good jobs will be the ones who acquire such skills. Everyone else will end up in service jobs.

The school that perhaps applies this philosophy most clearly is High Tech High, a school in San Diego. It was founded by business leaders to create business leaders. Qualcomm and a number of other local technology companies threw in the money, and it opened in September of 2000. San Diego is currently going through an economic transition as parts of its naval bases are being closed down and many technology companies that cannot afford to locate in Silicon Valley are coming in. Everything about the school connected it to the high-tech workplace. The architecture made it look like a typical dot-com company. The ceilings were completely opened, covered with exposed wires and pipes. A great room is built with 25 cubicle workstations. There are 12 seminar rooms where the walls can be moved around to facilitate team teaching. And there is a common room for socializing, meetings, and exhibitions of student work. The school is kept relatively small, consisting of 400 students in 2003. The school is organized around a set of projects in the first two years, and internships in the last two years. The projects are uploaded into digital portfolios and include work of varying quality. One project focused on genetic engineering describing and making use of various scientific tools. Another involved a four-person collaborative project on Magellan. Many of the projects are interdisciplinary, such as a robotics project that includes literature, physics, and computer science. The internships make the link between the school projects and the real world. One student was interning at a law firm that specialized in intellectual property. Others had students working with scientists or doctors. Students also met at school for internship seminars.

Basically, the school looks like the other constructivist technology environments we have been discussing. In all cases, it seems that the central pedagogical technique is to move students from the abstract to the concrete. At all of these schools, project-based learning, hands-on activities, and complex problem solving helped students grasp concepts that ordinarily might be classified as too advanced for them. And in all cases technology was just a part of the puzzle. It was the medium through which effective teachers helped students construct their own knowledge. And technology can be broadly construed. While all of the schools made use of computers to facilitate research, the presentation of work, and assessment without conventional testing, they also made use of more primitive technologies such as boats and moats. What comes through about the computers is their versatility, and that using them is less of a production than seeking petroglyphs on a raft or putting bacteria in an incubator. To be sure, multiple media should be used, but computers, by being in themselves a research tool, a presentation tool, a data analyzer, and an assessor, are a particularly efficient technology. This is perhaps one of the reasons that businesses, unlike schools, never debate about whether or not they should have computers and Web links; they are generally more concerned about how often to upgrade their hardware and software and how fast an Internet connection to support.

One anecdote from High Tech High makes clear how artificial the line is between school and work. Unlike the other schools studied, High Tech High had students' digital portfolios on the Web. (In the other schools, I either had to visit the school or order a CD.) Not only were the students identified on the Web site, but they included a resume. All of this might be seen by a school as the invasion of a student's privacy. But to the students it was a way to showcase their accomplishments so that colleges and employers could learn more about them, possibly having them for internships, thinking about college admissions, or even helping with a summer job. In this way the line between what is school and what is real life is more or less eliminated. And this creates a great potential for learning because it is the essence of higher order thinking. The real barrier that didactic environments create is that they make schools as different from the real world as possible when they should be as much like it as is developmentally appropriate.

KEY POINTS

- A case study of an unidentified urban high school indicated that the teacher used the computer lab as a dumping ground for students, having them use it for largely unsupervised drill-and-practice activities.
- A case study of the ALL school indicated that the use of technology is just a small part of a project-based, constructivist approach to learning.
- A case study of the Roots and Wings Community School indicated that technology was just one of many media employed to teach students in a constructivist fashion.
- A case study of King Middle School indicated that technology could take many forms besides computers.
- A case study of High Tech High indicated that technology could strengthen the connection between the school and the real world.

CHAPTER 4

The Effectiveness of Educational Technology: What the Numbers Say

Qualitative observations are useful in giving the research a sense of meaning. They illustrate precisely how technology can be used and whether those uses appear to promote student learning as observed in student work. Qualitative research, in a systematic way, provides a teacher or student with an outsider's view of the relative effectiveness or ineffectiveness of educational technology. And this kind of sharing of experiences between researcher and practitioner is absolutely necessary to the research endeavor. Without a common set of observations to draw upon, the practitioner will not know how the researcher is making sense out of the educational technology experiences. And only observations can provide sufficient richness to explain what the technology does and how it does it. For instance, the test scores used in quantitative research are but rough proxies of the portfolios of student work examined in the last chapter. And characterizing how a teacher uses technology on the basis of a few survey questions just scratches the surface of what can be learned by sitting in a classroom and observing its goings on.

All of that said, there are significant limitations of logic to what can be learned from qualitative research. It can establish that there exists a situation under which technology appears to work in a certain way. But it leaves two questions unanswered. First, to what extent is the researcher's perception of what is occurring accurate? Qualitative observations, even when conducted under some rubric or conceptual framework, still have a high level of subjectivity. Indeed, as was seen in the last chapter, I and another researcher could take the same student work and characterize it as low or high caliber. Second, how representative is the phenomenon under observation? In studying educational technology, this question applies to two types of observations: observations of how the technology is used and observations of the impact of this use on students. A particular use may be very common, very uncommon, or somewhere in the middle. Similarly, a particular use may prove effective for all students, or it may only benefit certain kinds of students in certain circumstances. For instance, is it fair to assume that if Urban High School was exposed to the teaching and technology of King Middle School, students would produce work of similar quality? The answer is that one cannot make this assumption without engaging in two phenomena of quantitative research: sampling and measurement.

One of the strengths of quantitative research is its ability to draw samples. If a researcher wanted to learn about the prevalence of hands-on learning in San Francisco, he or she could randomly select a set of students from across the city and ask them if they engaged in hands-on learning. Based upon the results of this small group, he or she could generalize to the entire city. A researcher also can make use of psychometrics to develop standardized measures of student academic performance or any particular instructional practice. If, for instance, he or she wanted to know whether students exposed to hands-on learning learned more science, he or she could ask all of the students in the sample the same question about whether they engaged in hands-on learning and then administer the same science test to all of them. Using tests in this way is what is meant by standardized testing; it is like measuring the height of all students with the same ruler. One wouldn't want to measure some students in centimeters and others in inches.

The National Assessment of Educational Progress (NAEP) provides a highly effective yardstick. Otherwise known as "the nation's report card," NAEP is administered in various subjects to nationally representative samples of 4th, 8th, and 12th graders every year or two. This practice has been occurring since 1969, so it has been possible to track student performance for more than 30 years, as well as make comparisons among various demographic subgroups of students. In terms of measurement, the NAEP tests are state of the art, meaning that they do not suffer from many of the limitations common to standardized tests. They are not purely multiple choice, but include items that ask students to show their work, for which partial credit is awarded. They are also designed to test as broad a range of skills and knowledge as possible—not just basic skills, but higher order thinking skills. The framework for reading, for instance, on which the reading assessments are based, asks students to analyze texts not only by identifying key pieces of information in them and summarizing them, but also to identify the author's intent in the passage and talk critically about the author's rhetorical effectiveness (National Assessment Governing Board, 2000). While constructing such sophisticated tests is expensive, the payoff is an assessment that will be sensitive not only to students' ability to learn basic facts, but also their ability to learn abstractions and apply them in complex problem solving. Both didactic and constructivist approaches can thus be put to the test.

In addition to having students take the test, NAEP includes questionnaires administered to students, teachers, and school administrators. The teacher questionnaire is administered to the teacher of the subject on which the student is being tested. The teacher answers questions not only on his or her background, but also on the practices in which he or she engages in the classroom, including the prevalence and use of technology. The student questionnaire includes questions on student background as well as the frequency with which the student uses computers at home or school. The school administrator questionnaire includes information on computer access. It is therefore possible, using the data, to quantify how often students use computers, how many computers are available, what they do with them, and how well trained their teachers are on them.

Using certain statistical techniques, it is also possible to measure the effectiveness of the various aspects of technology use. Using a battery of techniques (the simplest of which is called Ordinary Least Squares Regression, or OLS for short) one is able to relate a series of inputs to an output. The output, in this case, is student test scores. The inputs are the various instructional practices of interest, including technology uses and other constructivist and didactic practices discussed in the preceding chapter. In addition, student demographic background and teacher background are included as inputs. What OLS and more sophisticated statistical models allow one to do is relate the instructional practices to student test scores, taking into account student and teacher background. *Taking into account* means that if a relationship is identified between an instructional practice, say hands-on learning, and test scores, say in mathematics, it can be concluded that for two students of similar background with teachers of similar background, the student who is exposed to hands-on learning will outperform his or her peer in math.

In much of this chapter, I will examine the prevalence of various technology uses, how they have changed over time, and how they relate to student test performance in math, science, and reading. But as the qualitative observations made clear, it is not possible to pull technology use out of the context of the teacher's overall pedagogy. Since I am ultimately interested in knowing whether students perform better with teachers who use computers in a constructivist fashion, it is first important to demonstrate that nontechnological constructivist practices are superior to didactic ones in terms of improved student performance. Without knowing this, one might conclude that technology is the exception to the pedagogical rule; that by and large, students should be taught didactically, but if computers are used, then and only then is constructivism important. What I seek to demonstrate is that constructivism is always superior to didacticism, and that technology is a medium that is well-equipped to facilitate constructivist pedagogy.

WHAT NAEP SAYS ABOUT NONTECHNOLOGICAL INSTRUCTIONAL PRACTICES

As the review of the research literature on teacher effects makes clear, there is relatively little evidence that teacher background characteristics consistently boost test scores. The exceptions seem to be teacher knowledge, as measured by standardized test scores, and teacher course taking in the subject he or she is teaching. NAEP does not include a teacher test but it does include information on teacher's major (a proxy of course taking) as well as teacher's education level and years of experience. The data in math, science, and reading all indicate that teacher's education level is not associated with student test scores. Years of experience proves important for fourth graders in learning to read, but not in other subjects or grade levels, suggesting that teachers learn how to teach reading primarily on the job. In math and science, the opposite is the case. The only teacher characteristic associated with student performance is teacher major, indicating that students perform better in math and science (at both the fourth- and eighth-grade levels) when their teachers have taken substantial coursework in the area (teachers were considered as majors if they majored or minored in the subject at the undergraduate or graduate level or in education with a pedagogical focus on that subject). Thus in math and science, teachers need to enter the classroom comfortable with the subject matter.

In terms of instructional practice, the NAEP data consistently demonstrate that students perform better in classrooms possessing the characteristics of constructivism discussed earlier in the book. First and foremost of these is conveying higher order thinking skills. As previously discussed, higher order thinking skills involve making abstract concepts concrete through complex and/or real-world problem solving. In mathematics, one way that this could be measured by NAEP was by asking teachers how often they had students work on problems that involved multiple solutions. Teachers were also asked if they had students solve problems involving real-world situations, and if they had students engage in hands-on activities. All of these practices proved positively related to student performance. In addition, project-based learning, which provides a context for learning higher order thinking skills, proved beneficial. In contrast, teachers were asked about certain didactic practices, including solving routine problems and emphasizing math facts. These practices, in most cases, proved either unrelated or negatively related to student performance. And when teachers were asked about training, the ones who had received professional development in higher order thinking skills had higher performing students. In science, the picture proved similar. Activities that concretized or illustrated concepts proved associated with higher student performance. And project-based learning, which was found to be so helpful to the development of higher order thinking skills in the previous chapter, proved associated with higher achievement in science. The helpful activities also included hands-on learning and conducting data analysis. In terms of training, students benefited the most from having teachers trained in lab work, arguably the most common way to concretize scientific concepts and method. Finally, in reading, teaching metacognitive skills proved strongly associated with higher reading scores. Metacognitive skills involve thinking about how one reads for understanding; it is thus the humanities counterpart to higher order thinking in math and science. In addition, students learned to read better when the reading was less of a rote activity; students did better reading real books than basal readers, and writing about actual literature rather than doing writing exercises made up for the specific purpose of teaching writing.

The NAEP data also found support for the other aspects of constructivist pedagogy. Classroom testing proved detrimental in math, science, and reading at every grade level. In other words, students who tested less in school performed better on the NAEP test. This suggests that portfolios and other less obtrusive forms of assessment are preferable. The benefits of project-based learning further support the idea that students should be assessed on the basis of their ongoing work. The customization of instruction also proved important. Students performed better when their teachers had professional development in addressing special needs and teaching culturally diverse and English Language Learning students. This customization proved beneficial to all students, not just the targeted ones, suggesting that it is teachers individualizing their instruction that is important, not for whom they are individualizing it. Finally, working in groups or with partners proved beneficial in mathematics and science, indicating that collaborative learning, an important component of the constructivist approach, has value.

In sum, it seems that, across the board, constructivist practices raise test scores whereas didactic practices do not. Some practices that may be either constructivist or didactic, depending upon how they are done, did prove beneficial. Fourth graders who spent more time on task in math and science did better in those subjects than those who spent less time. But whether this time was used in a constructivist or didactic fashion is an unknown. Another practice where it is key to know how the time is being used is educational technology, the subject of the rest of this chapter.

TABLE 4.1. Technology Use by Eighth Graders in Math

	1996	*2000*	*% Change*
Availability in math class	11%	18%	38.89%
Frequency of use at school	29%	24%	-20.83%
Frequency of use at home	30%	49%	38.78%
Teacher's feeling of preparedness	55%	58%	5.17%
Types of use			
Drill and practice	16%	15%	-6.67%
Demonstrate new topics	4%	8%	50%
Play math games	13%	14%	7.14%
Simulations/ applications	12%	12%	0%
Don't use computer	54%	52%	-3.85%

EDUCATIONAL TECHNOLOGY IN MATHEMATICS

NAEP is administered every year or two, but the subjects vary and at times the grade levels vary. The grades are always some combination of 4th, 8th, and 12th, but some years only one of those grades will be surveyed, more usually all three. The mathematics assessment, which has been administered off and on since 1970, was administered in 1996 and 2000. (The most recent assessment was in 2003, but the data are not yet available for the kinds of statistical analyses performed here.) In the 1996 assessment, 6,000 fourth graders and 7,000 eighth graders were tested, and in the 2000 assessment, 13,000 fourth graders and 15,000 eighth graders were tested. Twelfth graders are not analyzed here because of statistical complications surrounding the use of such data. The math data made it possible to learn nine things about school technology use: how available the technology was in math class (two or more computers in a math classroom, one or less, or a separate lab); how often students used a computer for math in school (at least once a week); how often students used a computer for math at home (at least once a week); how prepared the teacher felt to use computers (very well prepared, well prepared, and so on), and how often computers were used for five types of use: drill and practice, demonstrating new topics, playing math games, conducting simulations or applications of math concepts, and not using computers at all. Frequency of student use was reported by students, and access, teacher preparedness, and types of use by teachers.

The results indicate a period of substantial change from 1996 to 2000—not surprising given the high level of policy attention paid to technology during that period (Table 4.1). From the eighth-grade data, one can see that the availability of enough computers in math class for students to engage in the kinds of constructivist activities described in the last chapter increased from 11% of students to 18% of students, about a 40% increase. While the increase is promising, the absolute number is still quite low. It is known that the average student to computer ratio is 5:1, which is small enough to permit constructivist activities. But many of those computers must be tucked away in labs, making it difficult for them to be integrated seamlessly into class time. It can thus be said that there may be enough computers in our schools, but not that they are properly placed. The amount of time students spent on computers at school actually decreased somewhat, by 20%. But this does not mean that students are using computers less; frequency of home use increased more than enough (40%) to compensate. So, as more students are getting computers in the home they are using them in schools less. This may suggest that teachers are assigning students more homework that involves computers, leaving less of it for class time. The absolute number for home use is striking; one out of two students use computers at home on a weekly or better basis to do math school work. Perhaps this is a tribute to effective marketing by computer manufacturers, to the increased affordability of computers, or to the emergence of laptop programs in which students get to take computers home with them. If the latter, the recent retrenchments of such programs may take a toll. There has been little change over time in teachers' feelings of preparedness. A little more than half of math teachers

TABLE 4.2. Technology Use by Fourth Graders in Math

	1996	2000	% Change
Availability in math class	28%	44%	36.36%
Frequency of use at school	34%	32%	-6.25%
Frequency of use at home	19%	23%	17.39%
Teacher's feeling of preparedness	58%	68%	14.71%
Types of use			
Drill and practice	27%	24%	-12.5%
Demonstrate new topics	2%	3%	33.33%
Play math games	41%	42%	2.38%
Simulations/ applications	6%	5%	-20%
Don't use computer	25%	26%	3.85%

feel well prepared to use computers. While the good news is that the glass is half full, it is also half empty. If one out of two teachers are uncomfortable with computers, they might not use them at all, or if they use them, will use them in ways where they themselves do not have to be involved. (Recall Urban High School.)

The types of use to which teachers put computers has been relatively stable over the years. The most frequent use was playing math games. Forty percent of teachers reported that they had students use computers primarily for this purpose. The next most frequent use was no use at all; 25% of teachers reported that they did not have students use computers. The next most frequent use was for drill and practice, with 15% of teachers saying this was the primary use to which they had students put computers. The two rarest uses were conducting simulations on applications and demonstrating new topics. These are the uses associated with higher order thinking skills; particularly, simulations and applications involve making concepts concrete. For instance, the ALL teacher who used a spreadsheet to teach algebra would fall into this category.

**TABLE 4.3. Links Between Technology Use and Math Scores
—Eighth Graders**

Variable	Effect on test scores
Frequency of school computer use	-.06**
Frequency of home computer use	.07**
Teacher computer preparedness	.05**
Use: simulations/applications	.04**
Use: drlll and practice	-.06**
Student socioeconomic status	.39**
Average class size	.06**
Teacher background	.05**

*p<.10; **p<.05.

It should be noted that there are substantial differences in patterns of computer use for different groups of students. The biggest divide is between urban and suburban schools. There is not much difference in access or frequency of use in school. These facts are testaments to the enormous amount of money spent bringing computers to schools. But there are vast divides in home use, teacher preparedness, and types of use. Urban students, minority students, and low-income students are much less likely than their suburban, white, and high-income counterparts to have computers at home. At school urban students are less likely to have teachers who feel well prepared (48% as opposed to 58%); the same holds for minority and low-income students. Finally, in terms of types of use, urban, minority, and low-income students are more likely to be exposed to drill-and-practice computer activities and less likely to be exposed to higher order activities.

For fourth graders in mathematics, patterns are largely the same (Table 4.2). Access increased between 1996 and 2000. About half of teachers feel well prepared, and the types of use remained stable. The differences in demographic groups, however, were much less pronounced. The big gap for fourth graders was in game playing, which high-income, white, suburban students engaged in more frequently than their low-income, minority, urban counterparts.

In relating all of these aspects of technology to student math performance, one clear finding came through: Students performed

**TABLE 4.4. Links Between Technology Use and Math Scores—
     Fourth Graders**

Variable	*Effect on Test Scores*
Frequency of school computer use	-.06**
Frequency of home computer use	-.10**
Teacher computer preparedness	.01
Use: games	.03*
Student socioeconomic status	.59**
Average class size	.07**
Teacher background	.01

*p<.10; **p<.05.

better when computers were used in a constructivist fashion (Tables 4.3 and 4.4). For both fourth and eighth graders, the frequency of school use proved negatively related to student performance. This means that students spending a great deal of time in school using computers are not using them productively. This should come as no surprise; in Urban High School the students filled the class time using computers for drills, but to little effect. In the constructivist classrooms, computers are just one piece of the puzzle, so in raw time, they are probably used less. Home use varied by grade: For fourth graders, time spent on computers had a negative effect, while for eighth graders, it had a positive effect. Perhaps fourth graders have more difficulty structuring their time on computers or tie it less to their subject than eighth graders. The importance of teacher preparedness also varied by grade: For fourth graders, it did not make a difference, whereas for eighth graders, it did. In eighth grade, students performed better when their teachers felt well prepared to use computers. In terms of types of use, one had an effect for fourth graders and two for eighth graders. For fourth graders, playing games seemed to be positively related to student test performance. For eighth graders, simulations and applications had a positive effect and drill and practice had a negative effect. For eighth graders the interpretation is straightforward: Computers are helpful when used in constructivist ways and harmful when used in didactic ways. For fourth graders, it may be that their relatively

TABLE 4.5. Technology Use by Eighth Graders in Science

	1996	2000	% Change
Availability in science class	n/a	20%	n/a
Frequency of use at school	15%	n/a	n/a
Frequency of use at home	33%	51%	55%
Professional development— Data analysis	51%	55%	8%
Professional development— Data acquisition	48%	60%	25%
Types of use			
Data analysis	19%	33%	74%
Drill and practice	8%	8%	0%
Play science/ learning games	21%	15%	-29%
Simulations and modeling	25%	23%	-8%
Word processing	22%	35%	59%

early stage in the mathematics curriculum makes games the only way to concretize math concepts while keeping student attention. Or it might mean that the positive effect of constructivist math on fourth graders does not work through the medium of technology.

EDUCATIONAL TECHNOLOGY IN SCIENCE

In science, it was possible to examine ten aspects of educational technology for 13,000 fourth graders and 15,000 eighth graders (albeit different samples for the two grades). These were access to two or more computers in the science classroom; frequency of school computer use (at least once a week); frequency of home computer use (at least once a week); professional development in

TABLE 4.6. Technology Use by Fourth Graders in Science

	1996	*2000*	*% Change*
Availability in science class	n/a	37%	n/a
Frequency of use at school	19%	n/a	n/a
Frequency of use at home	21%	25%	19%
Professional development— Data analysis	34%	48%	12%
Professional development— Data acquisition	31%	33%	6%
Types of use			
Data analysis	6%	9%	50%
Drill and practice	5%	3%	-40%
Play science/ learning games	30%	28%	-7%
Simulations and modeling	18%	11%	-39%
Word processing	10%	13%	30%

using computers for data analysis; professional development in using computers for data acquisition; and five types of use: data analysis, drill and practice, games, simulations and modeling, and word processing.

Starting again with the eighth graders, there was no 1996 measure of availability (Table 4.5). The 2000 measure indicates that one out of five students were in classes with at least two computers, the same as was the case in eighth-grade math. Regarding frequency of school use, there was no 2000 measure. The 1996 measure indicated about 15% of students using computers at least once a week in school. Interestingly this is about half the frequency of use found in math classes. One out of three students used computers at home at least once a week in 1996, and this amount increased substantially by 2000. About half of all eighth-grade teachers received the two forms

**TABLE 4.7. Links Between Technology Use and Science Scores—
Eighth Graders**

Variable	*Effect on test scores*
Frequency of school computer use	-12**
Frequency of home computer use	.04**
Teacher computer preparedness	.02**
Use: data analysis	.04**
Use: simulations	.07**
Student socioeconomic status	.54**
Average class size	.09**
Teacher background	-.01

*$p<.10$; **$p<.05$.

**TABLE 4.8. Links Between Technology Use and Science Scores—
Fourth Graders**

Variable	*Effect on test scores*
Frequency of school computer use	-.21**
Frequency of home computer use	.04**
Teacher computer preparedness	—
Use: Games	.07**
Use: Simulations	.08**
Use: Wordprocessing	.09**
Student socioeconomic status	.25**
Average class size	.06**
Teacher background	.01

*$p<.10$; **$p<.05$.

of professional development measured. In terms of types of use, the pattern is very different from math. In science, drill-and-practice was the rarest use. The others differ in the changes that took place between 1996 and 2000. Data analysis and word processing became much more frequent, and games and simulations less so. These patterns all prove largely the same for fourth graders (Table 4.6).

The ethnic, class, and urban/suburban divides proved similar to those in math. While there was not much difference in access or frequency of use, the types of use varied markedly. White, suburban, and affluent students were more likely to use computers for data analysis and simulations and less likely to use them for drill and practice. Again, it is the urban students who are "drilled and killed," while the suburban students use computers in a constructivist fashion.

The relationships between aspects of technology and science achievement in fourth and eighth grades were similar in science to what they were in math (Tables 4.7 and 4.8). Frequency of school use was negative in both grades whereas frequency of home use was positive. Teacher preparedness made a difference in eighth grade, with students performing better with teachers who had received professional development in computer use. It did not make a difference in fourth grade, however. Of the types of use, in eighth grade the two constructivist uses, simulations and data analysis, were associated with high science scores. In fourth grade, data analysis was also associated with high scores, but the other effective practice was learning games rather than simulations. Perhaps, as with math, the lower level of student cognitive development makes games a better concretizer than simulations.

EDUCATIONAL TECHNOLOGY IN READING

Finally, reading was analyzed for eighth graders who took the 1998 assessment. Seven measures of technology were available: computer access (two or more computers in a classroom), teacher preparedness for computer use, teacher preparedness for using computers for reading, teacher preparedness for using computers for writing, and four types of use: basic spelling and punctuation; software for reading instruction, software to read stories, and

TABLE 4.9. Technology Use by Eighth Graders in Reading

	1998
Availability in reading class	15%
Teacher preparedness for use	85%
Teacher preparedness for use in reading	50%
Teacher preparedness for use in writing	57%
Types of use	
Spelling, punctuation, grammar	19%
Computer software for reading instruction	7%
Read stories or do reading work on computer	26%
Write drafts or final versions on computer	19%

software to write drafts or final versions of papers. Computer access was about where it was in math and science, at 15% (Table 4.9). Teacher preparedness for overall use was quite high, at 85%, but specifically for reading and writing, it was about where it was in other subjects—half said yes, half said no. The most common use seems to be reading stories on the computer, followed by two word processing uses: spelling/punctuation and revising papers.

Unlike math and science, there are few substantial gaps by demographic group. As with math and science, access and frequency of school use are about equal among subgroups. There are gaps in teacher preparation, with Latino students at an advantage and African American and Asian American students at a disadvantage. And in terms of use, there are no substantial differences. Perhaps the reason for this is that the categories of use in reading tell us little about whether they are constructivist or not. As our discussion of constructivist reading instruction indicated, a focus on metacognitive skills is most characteristic of such a pedagogy. Yet there is no reason to think that using computers for reading stories, for instance, means that they will be read metacognitively or not. The only type of use that would seem to encourage metacognition is revising drafts on the computer. Aside from checking spelling

**TABLE 4.10. Links Between Technology Use and Reading Scores—
Eighth Graders**

Variable	Effect on Test Scores
Frequency of school computer use	-.02
Frequency of home computer use	-.07**
Teacher computer preparedness	.01**
Use: Reading	-.05**
Use: Writing	.06**
Use: Grammar/Punctuation	-.05**
Student socioeconomic status	.55**
Student reading background	.18**

*p<.10; **p<.05.*

and punctuation, which is another category, revising drafts may encourage students to think through how a piece of writing is structured.

Indeed, when relationships between aspects of technology and reading scores are measured, only revising drafts seems to have a positive effect (Table 4.10). Frequency of school use proved unrelated to reading scores. Frequency of home use actually has a negative relationship to reading scores. Teacher preparedness was related to reading scores, indicating students performed better in reading when their teachers had some kind of professional development on computers. Of the three uses, spelling/punctuation and reading stories have negative effects. So it is probably the case that, in reading, the role of computers as constructivist tools is somewhat more limited than in math and science; computers can help students organize and reorganize papers, teaching them about rhetorical structure, but when it comes to reading stories, a book will do better, and when it comes to spellcheck, students will learn how to spell better by checking their own spelling. When my writing teacher in college told me spellcheck was the bane of his existence, he may have been right.

KEY POINTS

- Unique among educational research on the effectiveness of technology, this study relates various uses of technology to academic achievement in a variety of subjects for national samples of students and teachers.
- The data indicate that, of the nontechnological instructional practices of teachers, it is primarily the constructivist ones that are associated with high student performance.
- In mathematics and science, computer use is positively associated with student performance when computers are used in a constructivist fashion, and is either unassociated or negatively associated with student performance when computers are used in a didactic fashion.
- In reading, inferences are somewhat more difficult to make but suggest that when students use computers for word processing for meta-analytic purposes, students perform better, and when they are used for spellchecking or reading stories, students perform worse.

CHAPTER 5

Preparing Students for the Twenty-First Century

Based upon the anecdotes and statistics presented in this book, there seems to be a clear message for policymakers and educators about the effectiveness of educational technology: It depends. When the technology is used in concert with constructivist teaching practices, students tend to perform well; and when it is used in concert with didactic teaching practices, they do not. This does not mean, however, that technology is a purely neutral medium, reflecting whatever is put into it. It seems, from many of the anecdotes, that not only does constructivist teaching encourage effective technology use, but also the availability of technology can expand opportunities for constructivist teaching. Certainly, as the example from Plato illustrates, even technology such as a stick and some dirt can be used in a constructivist fashion. But what PCs, the Internet, and multimedia provide is a wide range of media that support constructivist practice and do so with relatively little hassle. Critics of technology are fond of complaining when one of the computers in a lab reads "error 42." Something always seems to go wrong with computers, they say. But it has been my experience that even computer breakdowns provide a constructivist opportunity. Since many of the students are inevitably more knowledgeable about computers than the teachers, they get to save the day. And in terms of hassle, computers need to be compared to other constructivist activities, not to the alternative of chalk and talk. Is it so much more of a hassle to fix or switch computers than to build a medieval castle from scratch? All complex problem solving is just that—it involves solving a lot of different problems, some of them unanticipated. On the grand scale of things, crash-prone computers or slow Internet connections are still more efficient media than most of the other constructivist practices on the table. Thus the question posed in the introduction can be answered: The value-added of computers lies in the high level of efficiency with which they can convey higher order thinking skills. Since, at least if documents like the SCANS report can be believed, policymakers want schools to produce students with higher order thinking skills, school technology is the best way available to increase productivity. It might be more expensive than doing drills with paper and pencil, but such drills just don't create a twenty-first-century end product whereas computers, appropriately used, do.

Now that I have made clear my opinion on the matter, I should explain why I feel I have the right to express it with such force. The key is the quantitative material in Chapter 4. In Chapter 3, I related a number of observations. These may have made clear what is meant by effective technology use, and they may suggest that somewhere, somehow, technology is being used in these ways. But critics of technology as well as advocates of replacing teachers with computers, as well as advocates of using computers for drills, all have their anecdotes too. Sometimes, we even look at the same work and reach different judgments.

The virtue of nationally representative quantitative data is that it is not just another field observation. It tells educators what is actually happening across the country. And it quantifies it. We now know how often students use computers for drill and practice and how often they use them to learn higher order thinking skills. And we know that students who use computers in the latter way perform better in math, science, and reading, regardless of demographic background or grade level. The federal government deserves credit for having collected the data needed to know these things almost every year for the last three decades. Since 1969 it has collected quantitative data on 4th, 8th, and 12th graders in various subjects as well as on their teachers and schools through NAEP.

Unfortunately, the future of this kind of quantitative educational research is in some doubt. The National Assessment Governing Board (NAGB), the federal agency that oversees NAEP, has decided to eliminate many of the questions asked of students, teachers, and schools, including the ones on technology. This means that this window into effective technology is going to close. That is a real loss, particularly given the nature of technology. Technology changes quickly, and what was effective in 2000 might not be effective in 2010. And if there is no national data, then educators will have to go back to confronting one another with anecdotes, or with studies of this or that innovative school district (studies which are also anecdotes). It will not be possible to see the extent to which our own experiences as educators typify the country as a whole or not.

What justification does NAGB provide for eliminating the data used for studies such as this? Members of the board and some of their research consultants point out that NAEP data are *cross-sectional*, meaning that the information about students, teachers, and schools is collected at the same time as students take the test. Consequently, it cannot be known for certain what the "causal direction" is for relationships discovered in the data. Does constructivist technology use raise student achievement scores, or are teachers simply more likely to use technology in a constructivist manner with their better students? It is true that educators can't know the answer to this for certain in a cross-sectional study. But we can't know this for certain in a *longitudinal* study, which collects data over time, either. In a longitudinal study, rather than associating technology use to student performance, we would be able to associate technology use to growth in student performance. But the same objection can be raised here. Do we know that constructivist technology use increases performance growth or that teachers use constructivist technology for students who tend to improve quickly academically? We can only solve the problem of cross-sectionality by doing random experiments, and those themselves are anecdotes; they can only be done for small groups of students in small numbers of schools because most parents don't want their children to be experimented on, or if they let their children participate, they want them to be exposed to the intervention rather than the placebo. For example, one of the most ambitious educational experiments of all time, the STAR experiment in Tennessee, actually managed to randomly place students in small or large classes and compare their test scores (Achilles & Finn, 2002). But after a year, parents were in an uproar, and the students in large classes got extra teacher's aides. After another couple of years, parents were so upset that the experiment had to be ended. So cross-sectional databases like NAEP are usually the only way we are going to be able to learn which instructional practices are associated with high student achievement, and without them we will be left in the dark.

So what is the answer to NAGB's challenge? How do educators make use of nationally representative data in a way that provides useful information without overselling the data? The answer is twofold: avoid causal explanations, and test data with experience. First, educators need to avoid explanations where the causal direction is of crucial importance. In this case, what I substantiated with the national data is that students in classrooms with constructivist computer uses outperform their peers in classrooms with didactic uses. This is a fact regardless of whether the computers caused the high performance or the students and/or their teachers tended to use computers in these ways. Next, educators should try plunking constructivist computers down in low-performing classrooms and see if anything happens. Here is where experience comes in. I have observed such classrooms, and the students do indeed perform well. The Worcester, New Mexico, Maine, and San Diego students were not from high-performing populations. Yet the quality of their work seemed high. So my experience would lead me to think that the associations I uncovered with national data do show a positive technology effect.

THE DIGITAL DIVIDE AND NO CHILD LEFT BEHIND

The data presented in Chapter 4 provide a new understanding of the digital divide. The *digital divide* refers to the gap in computer access between affluent and poor, or white and minority, students. For years, it was commonly believed that poor and minority students were behind in access to computers. And in response, the federal government, state governments, and corporations provided money to school systems to buy computers and connect them to the Internet. Now the student-computer ratios are the same for white and minority students (about 5:1) and the NAEP data reveal that white and minority students use computers with equal frequency. These findings are a testament to the ability of our society to equalize a resource when it puts its mind to it.

But society did not eliminate the digital divide where it really matters: in how computers are used. The research in Chapter 4 indicated that it was not the quantity but the quality of computer use that makes a difference to student achievement. If a teacher gives students the entire class time to work on computers, as the teacher in Urban High School did, that does not benefit the students if they are using the computers in unproductive ways. The key to using computers to increase student productivity is to have them used in a constructivist manner. But, as I said in Chapter 4, this is precisely the gap between minority and white students. Minority students are less likely to be exposed to those computer uses associated with high academic performance.

Current policy directs education to go beyond discussion of the digital divide in closing the achievement gap. The *achievement gap* is the difference in academic performance between white and minority students. According to NAEP, in math, science, and reading, minority performance has trailed white performance since 1969. While the gap closed somewhat during the 1970s and early 1980s, when policymakers were focusing on issues of equity, the gap widened during the 1990s, when policymakers focused on increasing excellence. NCLB legislation targets this gap to disappear. Individual schools would be expected to show improvements in student performance for all races, and all students, regardless of race, would be expected to meet a standard of proficiency by 2014.

Current legislation leans toward using didactic practices to close the gap. In reading, NCLB specifically calls for teaching phonics and providing grants to cities that emphasize basic skills approaches in math, science, and reading. However, NAEP data show that these practices are not necessarily the best ones to improve minority performance. Constructivist practices are not just good for white students; they are good for all students. And specifically in the case of educational technology, the way to use computers to close the gap is to give minority students more exposure to constructivist uses, not less. With the narrowing of the divide in computer use would come a narrowing of the achievement gap. And then, maybe some of the techno-skeptics would come around.

In sum, teaching and the media used with it are inseparable. Teachers cannot teach without having some means at their disposal to communicate their knowledge to their students. Technology, it appears, is a fine medium, provided teachers are up to the task. Being up to the task means that they are comfortable enough with both computers and the material to teach it in a constructivist rather than a didactic fashion. Given that present federal policy supports didacticism over constructivism, it is possible that there will be some support for professional development in using computers, but not in constructivist teaching methods. Consequently, if states, localities, and the private sector want the huge amounts of technology already in our schools used productively, they are going to have to buck the federal trend and invest in the kind of learning the CEO Forum and the SCANS report identified as valuable—a focus on higher order thinking skills and complex problem solving. When the federal government told New York City that it would need to adopt a basic skills reading curriculum to receive federal professional development money, it agreed—to the detriment of its students; for example, the city was forced to replace real books with basal readers, which NAEP research shows is a move in the wrong direction. It does not make sense for jurisdictions to accept money for training and curriculum that they know isn't very useful and that research shows is counterproductive. States, localities, and private foundations must take the lead in moving schools down the constructivist path if they want to see their students prepared for the twenty-first-century workforce.

KEY POINTS

- The data used in this study are at risk, making it unlikely that it will ever be replicated. The National Assessment Governing Board has decided to eliminate most of the background questions in NAEP, which would leave educators in the dark about the effectiveness of different uses of technology.
- The data indicate that the real digital divide is between the constructivist uses to which white, affluent, and suburban students are exposed and the didactic uses to which minority, poor, and urban students are exposed.
- This digital divide reflects an intentional policy on the part of

the Bush administration, which believes that minority students would be better served by didactic pedagogy.

- Given that the federal government favors more didactic forms of pedagogy, states, localities, and the private sector need to step up to the plate to support constructivist technology uses in inner-city schools so that these schools can produce a twenty-first-century workforce.

APPENDIX

How the Study Was Conducted

In seeking to identify differences between groups in aspects of technology use this study tested three sets of hypotheses. The first set of hypotheses concerned actual use of computers. First, it was hypothesized that due to enormous government investments in hardware there would be few significant differences in access to computers or frequency of use of computers at school. Because purchasing computers for the home has been found to be a good proxy of SES, and government investment in providing home computers (e.g., free laptop programs) has been modest, it was hypothesized next that more significant differences would exist in access at home, with affluent groups having more access than less affluent groups. It was also hypothesized that there would be significant differences in teacher preparedness to use computers, based on the fact that governments have spent less money proportionately on teacher training than on hardware, and consequently access to teachers with high levels of computer proficiency would be lower for students attending schools with fewer resources, generally less affluent students. Finally, it was hypothesized that there would be significant differences in the types of use to which computers are put, based on the notion that teachers in less affluent schools are more likely to use drill-and-practice uses and less likely to use higher order uses. This is the case for two reasons: They are encouraged to emphasize basic skills because it is believed that their student bodies cannot handle higher order uses, and they are more likely to lack the professional development needed to use educational technology in more advanced ways.

The second set of hypotheses concerned the relationship between the various aspects of technology and student academic performance in math, science, and reading. The study first expected that measures of the quantity of technology use would have a negligible or even negative relationship to student performance, the rationale being that the educational nature of computers depends upon what students are doing with them rather than how long they are doing it. Consequently, the study also expected that certain uses of computers—particularly those involving higher order

85

thinking skills—would have a positive effect on student performance across subjects. In addition, it was expected that better trained teachers, because they were more capable of engaging in the higher order uses, would have higher performing students.

The final set of hypotheses concerned the link between the digital divide and the aspects of computer use associated with high student performance. It was hypothesized that it was precisely those aspects of use—teacher preparedness and higher order uses—that would evince the largest digital divide. In other words, students from disadvantaged groups would be the least likely to be exposed to effective uses of technology.

To test these hypotheses, data were taken from the National Assessment of Educational Progress. Also known as "the nation's report card," NAEP administers an assessment in various subjects every year or two to nationally representative samples of 4th, 8th, and 12th graders. The assessments are used to track student performance over time and to compare performance among subgroups of students. In addition to the assessment, each administration of NAEP includes questionnaires sent to students, teachers, and school administrators (NCES, 1999). In Chapter 4, this study also attempted to test its first set of hypotheses by examining data from the 2000 NAEPs in math and science for 4th and 8th graders and the 1998 NAEP in reading for 8th graders. In Chapter 4, the study also attempted to test its second set of hypotheses by examining data from the 1996 NAEPs in math and science for 4th and 8th graders and the 1998 NAEP in reading for 8th graders. The teacher questionnaires included information on the types on technology use and the level of teacher preparedness; the student questionnaires included information on frequency of use as well as student background characteristics; and the school questionnaire included information on computer access. Teacher background and class size also came from the teacher questionnaire.

For the first set of hypotheses (Chapter 3) scores on the various aspects of technology were compared for subgroups. The subgroups were: men and women; whites, African Americans, Latinos, and Asian Americans; those eligible and ineligible for free or reduced-price lunches; those in public and private schools; those in urban, suburban, and rural schools; and those in the northeast, southeast, central, and western regions of the country. Differences were tested for statistical significance using t tests for two-group comparisons and Bonferonni tests for multiple-group comparisons. Differences of 3% or greater were deemed substantively significant. Only differences that proved substantial in both of these ways were treated as different.

For the second set of hypotheses, a series of structural equation models was developed. Structural equation modeling (SEM) involves two components: path models and factor models. The factor models reduce a series of indicators, referred to as *manifest variables*, into a construct, known as a *latent variable*. Thus, SES, a latent variable, can be generated from measures of parents' education and possessions in the home. Latent variables can even be constructed with single indicators, by setting the error term (variable variance unexplained by the latent variable) to zero and setting the coefficient relating the two variables to one. The path models then relate the latent variables to one another (Arbuckle, 1997; Gustafsson & Stahl, 1997; Hayduk, 1987; Jöreskog & Sörbom, 1993).

Structural equation models have certain advantages over standard regression models that made it important to use them for these analyses. First, some of the latent variables could only be constructed through multiple indicators, including SES. Second, the model hypothesized not only that a series of independent variables would be related to a dependent variable, but that many variables would act both as independent and dependent variables. For instance, uses of technology were expected to both affect student performance and be affected by professional development. While a series of regression equations can also accomplish this, SEM provides for statistical tests for the overall fit of the model, which regressions cannot. Overall model fit is tested by a series of indices known as *goodness-of-fit indices*, where models are deemed acceptable with scores of .9 or better, and the root mean squared errors of approximation, where models are deemed acceptable with scores below .05.

For this analysis certain adaptations needed to be made to conform to the design of the NAEP data. First, the NAEP test scores are calculated as what are known as five *plausible values*. Because each student answers a relatively small number of items on the assessment, the final score needs to be imputed. Ordinary item response theory parameters are not sufficient and consequently imputations are generated by making different assumptions about various background variables. These assumptions result in the five values. To analyze these values, it is necessary to conduct five separate analyses, one corresponding to each plausible value. The results of the five analyses can then be combined through a series of formulas. Second, the sampling design of NAEP is stratified and clustered. Consequently, standard errors calculated as if the sample is a simple random one are underestimates. NAEP includes a set of weights, known as *jackknife weights*, to take this into account. Because of the computational expense of using jackknife weights (56 models would be required for each of the five models) design effect methodology was employed instead. *Design effects* are coefficients that are calculated by estimating the ratio between a jackknife weighted and unweighted path model parameter, and inflating all standard errors by that ratio (Johnson, 1989; Johnson, Mislevy, & Thomas, 1994; O'Reilly, Zelenak, Rogers, & Kline, 1996). In total, 25 models were run. Five models were run for each sample, and there were five samples: fourth-grade math, fourth-grade science, eighth-grade math, eighth-grade science, and eighth-grade reading. The results from these models are presented in Chapter 4.

The final hypothesis was not formally tested. Rather, as the conclusion indicated, the effective aspects of technology were indeed the ones to which disadvantaged students were less likely to be exposed. This conclusion was drawn by matching the results of Chapter 3 with those of Chapter 4.

A word is in order about using NAEP data to draw causal inferences. NAEP data are cross-sectional, and consequently the independent and dependent variables are observed at about the same time. As a result, relationships uncovered in the data can go in one of two causal directions: either variable could be the dependent one. For instance, if higher order thinking skills are associated with student performance, it could be that higher order thinking skills raise performance, or it could be that higher performing students are more likely to receive exposure to higher order thinking skills. Given this ambiguity, what is the use of secondary analyses of NAEP data?

The answer is that while NAEP data cannot be used in a vacuum to demonstrate causal relationships, it can be used to test such relationships uncovered by other work. If small-scale studies have found teacher training in technology to be associated with higher student performance, this proposition can be tested using NAEP data. It would be expected that the NAEP data would find a positive relationship. If they did, the hypothesis would be confirmed.

NAEP data possess certain advantages over smaller scale data that make it worth this trouble. Small-scale data often possess the advantage of being experimental or quasi-experimental, which means they have a high degree of internal validity. It is not known, however, how the results of such a study would look with different subjects or a different program. What is true for 40 male college students may not be true for the population as a whole, and, in replicating the intervention with a different group, it would need to be implemented in every detail, as it is not known which components of the program made a difference. NAEP has the virtue of being the only database that can, year after year, test hypotheses for a nationally representative sample of students and schools and thus be generalizable to the nation. While NAEP's internal validity is low, its external validity is as high as it can get in studying U.S. education.

In addition, certain variables in NAEP make it possible to get a sense of the causal direction of independent and dependent variables. In reading, it is possible to take into account a student's prior reading level as measured by a series of indicators. In math, it is possible to see the level of difficulty of the class in which the student was placed, also suggesting something about the student's prior ability. Given that the link between the relevant technology aspects and achievement were not sensitive to the inclusion of these variables, it suggests that the technology aspects have an impact on achievement rather than the other way around.

Another cautionary note about the methodology of the study. The study utilizes SEM, a regression-type technique. While the technique possesses many advantages over conventional regression, it does not directly take into account the multiple levels of analysis involved in the analysis of school data. The NAEP data occur at multiple levels; many of the independent variables are at the school level, whereas the dependent variable is at the student level. While the use of design effects takes the clustered nature of the sample into account in adjusting standard errors, it does not explicitly model this clustering. Thus, some technique that both had the advantages of SEM and took into account the multilevel nature of the data would be preferable.

References

Achilles, C., & Finn, J. (2002). Making sense of continuing and renewed class-size. Washington, DC: ERIC.

American Federation for Teachers. (1999). *Making standards matter: An update on state activity* (Educational Issues Policy Brief No. 11). Retrieved Ocotober 5, 2004, from http://www.aft.org/pubs-reports/downloads/teachers/policy11.pdf

American Institutes for Research. (1999). *An educators' guide to schoolwide reform.* Arlington, VA: Educational Research Service.

Arbuckle, J. L. (1997). *Amos users' guide, version 3.6.* Chicago: Small Waters Corporation.

Archer, J. (2000). The link to higher scores. In R. D. Pea, *The Jossey-Bass Reader on Technology and Learning.* Indianapolis, IN: Jossey-Bass.

Babbie, E. (2002). *The basics of social research.* Belmont, CA: Wadsworth/Thomson Learning.

Baird, W. E., & Koballa, T. R. (1986). Changes in preservice elementary teachers' hypothesizing skills and selected attitudes following group and individual study with computer-presented text or computer simulation. (ERIC Document No. ED266946)

Baker, E. L., Gearhart, M., & Herman, J. L. (1993). *The Apple classrooms of tomorrow: The UCLA evaluation studies* (CSE Technical Report No. 353). Los Angeles: University of California–Los Angeles, Center for the Study of Evaluation/Center for Technology Assessment.

Barton, P. E., Coley, R. J., & Wenglinsky, H. (1998). *Order in the classroom: Violence, discipline and student achievement.* Princeton, NJ: Educational Testing Service.

Berends, M., Bodilly, S., & Kirby, S. N. (2002). *Facing the challenges of whole-school reform: New American Schools after a decade.* Santa Monica, CA: RAND.

Bill & Melinda Gates Foundation. (2003). *Grant highlights.* Retrieved October 5, 2004 from http://www.gatesfoundation.org/grants

Borja, R. R. (2002, May 9). One state's digital quest. *Technology Counts 2002, 21* (35), 47–52.

Burns, P., & Bozeman, W. (1981). Computer-assisted instruction and mathematics achievement: Is there a relationship? *Educational Technology, 21,* 32–39.

Carnegie Forum on Education and the Economy. (1986). *A nation prepared: Teachers for the twenty-first century. The report of the Task Force on Teaching as a Profession.* Washington, DC: Author.

CEO Forum on Education and Technology. (1997). *From pillars to progress.* Washington, DC: CEO Forum.

CEO Forum on Education and Technology. (1999). *Professional development: A link to better learning.* Washington, DC: CEO Forum.

CEO Forum on Education and Technology. (2000). *The power of digital learning: Integrating content.* Washington, DC: CEO Forum.

CEO Forum on Education and Technology. (2001). *Key building blocks for student achievement in the twenty-first century: Assessment, alignment, accountability, access, and analysis.* Washington, DC: CEO Forum.

Christmann, E., Badgett, J., & Lucking, R. (1997). Progressive comparison of the effects of computer assisted instruction on the academic achievement of secondary students. *Journal of Research on Computing in Education, 29*(4), 325–337.

Clark, R. E. (1984). Research on student thought processes during computer-based instruction. *Journal of Instructional Development, 7,2–5.*

Colorado, R. J. (1988). Computer-assisted instruction research: A critical assessment. *Journal of Research on Computing in Education, 20,* 226–233.

Cordes, C., & Miller, E. (Eds.). (2000). *Fool's gold: A critical look at computers in childhood.* College Park, MD: Alliance for Childhood.

Cuban, L. (1986). *Teachers and machines: The classroom use of technology since 1920.* New York: Teachers College Press.

Cuban, L. (2001). *Oversold and underused: Computers in the classroom.* Cambridge, MA: Harvard University Press.

Danielson, C. (1996). *Enhancing professional practice: A framework for teaching.* Alexandria, VA: Association for Supervision and Curriculum and Development.

Dence, M. (1980). Toward defining the role of CAI: A review. *Educational Technology, 20,* 50-54.

Driscoll, R. E. (1990). *A comparison of the relative effectiveness of microcomputer-assisted instruction and conventional instruction for the teaching of reference skills to seventh-grade students.* Unpublished doctoral dissertation, University of Connecticut, Storrs.

Final fiscal 2001 appropriations and President Bush's fiscal 2002 proposals. (2001, May 16). *Education Week, 20*(36), 1–2.

Forman, D. (1982, January). Search of the literature. *The Computing Teacher, 9,* 37–51.

Gustafsson, J. E., & Stahl, P. A. (1997). *STREAMS user's guide, version 1.7.* Mölndal, Sweden: Multivariate Ware.

Hamilton, E., & Cairns, H. (Eds.). (1987). *The collected dialogues of Plato, including the letters* (W.K.C. Guthrie, Trans.). Princeton, NJ: Princeton University Press.

Hayduk, L. A. (1987). *Structural equation modeling with LISREL: Essentials and advances.* Baltimore, MD: Johns Hopkins University Press.

Holmes Group, Inc. (1986). *Tomorrow's teacher: A report of the Holmes Group.* East Lansing, MI: Author.

Intel Corporation. (2004). Intel in your community [http://www.intel.com/ community].

Johnson, E. (1989). Considerations and techniques for the analysis of NAEP data. *Journal of Education Statistics, 14*(4), 303–334.

Johnson, E., Mislevy, R. J., & Thomas, N. (1994). Scaling procedures. In E. Johnson & J. Carlson, *The NAEP 1992 technical report* (pp. 241–256). Princeton, NJ: Educational Testing Service.

Jöreskog, K. G., & Sörbom, D. (1993). *Structural equation modeling and the SIMPLIS command language.* Chicago: Scientific Software International.

Kulik, C. C., & Kulik, J. A. (1991). Effectiveness of computer-based instruction: An updated analysis. *Computers in Human Behavior, 7*(1–2), 75–94.

Kulik, J.A., Bangert-Drowns, R., & Williams G. (1983). Effects of computer-based teaching on secondary students. *Journal of Educational Psychology, 75*, 19–26.

Kulik, J. A., Kulik, C. C., & Cohen, P. A. (1980). Effectiveness of computer-based college teaching: A meta-analysis of findings. *Review of Educational Research, 50*(4), 525–544.

Levin, H. M., Glass, G., & Meister, G. (1987). Cost-effectiveness of computer-assisted instruction. *Evaluation Review, 11*(1), 50–72.

Liao, Y. K. (1992). Effects of computer-assisted instruction on cognitive outcomes: A meta-analysis. *Journal of Research on Computing in Education, 24*(3), 367–380.

Linn, M., & His, S. (2000). *Computers, teachers, peers: Science learning partners.* Mahwah, NJ: Lawrence Erlbaum Associates.

Mann, D., Shakeshaft, C., Becker, J., & Kottkamp, R. (1999). *West Virginia's basic skills/computer education program: An analysis of student achievement.* Santa Monica, CA: Milken Family Foundation.

Maryland Mathematics Commission. (2001). *Keys to math success.* Baltimore, MD: Maryland Department of Education.

Merchilinsky, S. (2001). *The 1996 Technology Innovation Challenge Grant projects: Highlights from the interim reviews.* Washington, DC: U.S. Department of Education.

Meyer, L. (2001). Technology Counts 2001 [Special edition]. *Education Week, 20*(35).

National Assessment Governing Board. (2000). *Reading framework for the National Assessment of Education Progress: 1992–2000.* Washington, DC: U.S. Department of Education.

National Association of State Boards of Education (NASBE). (2001). *Any time, any place, any path, any pace: Taking the lead on e-learning policy.* Washington, DC: Author.

National Center for Education Statistics. (NCES). (1996). *Pursuing excellence: A study of U.S. eighth grade mathematics and science teaching, learning, curriculum and achievement in international context.* Washington, DC: U.S. Government Printing Office.

National Center for Education Statistics. (NCES). (1997). *Pursuing excellence: A study of U.S. fourth grade mathematics and science achievement in international context.* Washington, DC: U.S. Government Printing Office.

National Center for Education Statistics. (NCES). (1998). *Pursuing excellence: A study of U.S. twelfth grade mathematics and science achievement in international context.* Washington, DC: U.S. Government Printing Office.

National Center for Education Statistics. (NCES). (1999). *The NAEP 1996 technical report.* Washington, DC: U.S. Government Printing Office.

National Center for Education Statistics. (2000). *NAEP 1999 Trends in academic progress.* Washington, DC: U.S. Government Printing Office.

National Commission on Excellence in Education. (1983). *A nation at risk: The imperative for educational reform.* Washington, DC: U.S. Government Printing Office.

National Commission on Teaching and America's Future (NCTAF). (1996). *What matters most: Teaching for America's future.* New York: Author.

National Council of Teachers of Mathematics (NCTM). (1989). *Curriculum and evaluation standards for school mathematics.* Reston, VA: Author.

National Council on the Accreditation of Teacher Education (NCATE). (2003). *A decade of growth 1991–2001.* Retrieved October 5, 2004, from http://www.ncate.org/newsbrfs/dec_report.htm

National Science Teachers Association. (1997). *National science education standards.* Washington, DC: Author.

Niemiec, R. P., Samson, G., Weinstein, T., & Walberg, H. (1987). The effects of computer-based instruction in elementary schools: A quantitative synthesis. *Journal of Research on Computing in Education, 19*(2), 263–276.

Niemiec, R. P., & Walberg, H. J. (1989). From teaching machines to microcomputers: Some milestones in the history of computer-based instruction. *Journal of Research on Computing in Education, 21*(3), 263–276.

Oppenheimer, T. (2003). *The flickering mind: The false promise of technology in the classroom and how learning can be saved.* New York: Random House.

O'Reilly, P. E., Zelenak, C. A., Rogers, A. M., & Kline, D. L. (1996). *1994 trial state assessment program in reading secondary-use data files user guide.* Washington, DC: U.S. Department of Education.

Ravitch, D. (1995). *National standards in American education: A citizen's guide.* Washington, DC: Brookings Institution.

Rousseau, J. J. (2003). *Emile* (P. D. Jimack, Trans.). London: Everyman. (Original work published 1762)

Sandham, J. L. (2001, May 10, 2001). Across the nation. Technology Counts 2001 [special edition]. *Education Week, 20*(35), 67–68.

Sandholtz, J. H., Ringstaff, C., Dwyer, D. C. (1997). *Teaching with technology: Creating student-centered classrooms.* New York: Teachers College Press.

Secretary's Commission on Achieving Skills. (1992). *What work requires of schools.* Washington, DC: U.S. Department of Labor.

Stigler, J. W., & Hiebert, J. (1999). *The teaching gap: Best ideas from the world's teachers for upcoming education in the classroom.* New York: The Free Press.

Suppes, P., & Morningstar, M. (1968). Computer-assisted instruction. *Science, 166,* 343–350.

Trotter, A. (1997, November 10). Taking technology's measure. Technology

Counts 1997 [special edition]. *Education Week, 17*(11), 6–11.

Tucker, M. S., & Codding, J. B. (1998). *Standards for our schools: How to set them, measure them and reach them.* San Francisco, CA: Jossey-Bass.

U.S. Department of Education. (1996). *Getting America's students ready for the twenty-first century: Meeting the technology literacy challenge.* Retrieved October 5, 2004, from http://www.ed.gov/technology/plan/nattechplan.

U.S. Department of Education. (2000). *E-learning: Putting a world-class education at the fingertips of all children.* Washington, DC: U.S. Government Printing Office.

U.S. Department of Education. (2003a). *Enhancing education through technology.* Retrieved October 5, 2004, from www.ed.gov/legislation/lesea02/pg34.html

U.S. Department of Education. (2003b). *Improving America's Schools Act of 1994.* Retrieved October 5, 2004, from http://www.ed.gov/legislation/ESEA/sec3111.html.

U.S. Department of Education. (2003c). Overview: Introduction: *No Child Left Behind.* Retrieved October 5, 2004, from http://www.ed.gov/nclb/overview/intro/index.html

U.S. Department of Education. (2004). Preparing Tomorrow's Teachers to Use Technology Program. [http://www.ed.gov/programs/teachtech/pt3faqs03.html]

Web-Based Education Commission. (2001). *Moving from promise to practice: Report of the Web-Based Education Commission to the President and the Congress of the United States.* Washington, DC: U.S. Government Printing Office.

Wenglinsky, H. (1998). *Does it compute? The relationship between educational technology and student achievement in mathematics.* Princeton, NJ: Educational Testing Service.

Index

About the Author

Harold Wenglinsky received his Ph.D. in sociology from New York University in 1996. An expert on the quantitative analysis of large-scale data to answer questions of educational policy, Wenglinsky was appointed National Assessment of Educational Progress (NAEP) Visiting Scholar at Educational Testing Service (ETS) that year, and went on to become a research scientist and then director of the ETS Policy Information Center. He then became an associate professor at the School of Public Affairs at Baruch College as well as the Graduate Center of the City University of New York. He later transferred to Hunter College of the City University of New York, where he was an associate professor in the School of Education and the director of Assessment and Accreditation. He recently testified before the National Assessment Governing Board on the importance of NAEP for studying issues of educational policy and continues to advocate for the secondary analysis of NAEP data as a member of the American Educational Research Association Governmental Relations Committee. Currently, Dr. Wenglinsky is a research manager for the Grow Network/McGraw-Hill.